MznLnx

Missing Links Exam Preps

Exam Prep for

Managerial Accounting

Hansen & Mowen, 8th Edition

The MznLnx Exam Prep is your link from the texbook and lecture to your exams.
The MznLnx Exam Preps are unauthorized and comprehensive reviews of your textbooks.

All material provided by MznLnx and Rico Publications (c) 2010
Textbook publishers and textbook authors do not particpate in or contribute to these reviews.

MznLnx

Rico Publications

Exam Prep for Managerial Accounting
8th Edition
Hansen & Mowen

Publisher: Raymond Houge
Assistant Editor: Michael Rouger
Text and Cover Designer: Lisa Buckner
Marketing Manager: Sara Swagger
Project Manager, Editorial Production: Jerry Emerson
Art Director: Vernon Lowerui

Product Manager: Dave Mason
Editorial Assitant: Rachel Guzmanji
Pedagogy: Debra Long
Cover Image: Jim Reed/Getty Images
Text and Cover Printer: City Printing, Inc.
Compositor: Media Mix, Inc.

(c) 2010 Rico Publications
ALL RIGHTS RESERVED. No part of this work
covered by the copyright may be reproduced or
used in any form or by an means--graphic, electronic,
or mechanical, including photocopying, recording,
taping, Web distribution, information storage, and
retrieval systems, or in any other manner--without the
written permission of the publisher.

Printed in the United States
ISBN:

For more information about our products, contact us at:
Dave.Mason@RicoPublications.com

For permission to use material from this text or
product, submit a request online to:
Dave.Mason@RicoPublications.com

Contents

CHAPTER 1
Introduction: The Role, History, and Direction of Management Accounting   1

CHAPTER 2
Basic Management Accounting Concepts   10

CHAPTER 3
Activity Cost Behavior   16

CHAPTER 4
Activity-Based Product Costing   21

CHAPTER 5
Activity-Based Management   25

CHAPTER 6
Job-Order and Process Costing   29

CHAPTER 7
Support-Department Cost Allocation   34

CHAPTER 8
Budgeting for Planning and Control   40

CHAPTER 9
Standard Costing: A Managerial Control Tool   47

CHAPTER 10
Segmented Reporting, Investment Center Evaluation, and Transfer Pricing   51

CHAPTER 11
Cost-Volume-Profit Analysis: A Managerial Planning Tool   57

CHAPTER 12
Tactical Decision Making   62

CHAPTER 13
Capital Investment Decisions   68

CHAPTER 14
Inventory Management   78

CHAPTER 15
Quality Costs and Productivity: Measurement, Reporting, and Control   84

CHAPTER 16
Lean Accounting, Target Costing, and the Balanced Scorecard   88

CHAPTER 17
Environmental Cost Management   95

CHAPTER 18
International Issues in Management Accounting   99

ANSWER KEY   106

TO THE STUDENT

COMPREHENSIVE

The *MznLnx* Exam Prep series is designed to help you pass your exams. Editors at MznLnx review your textbooks and then prepare these practice exams to help you master the textbook material. Unlike study guides, workbooks, and practice tests provided by the texbook publisher and textbook authors, *MznLnx* gives you **all** of the material in each chapter in exam form, not just samples, so you can be sure to nail your exam.

MECHANICAL

The MznLnx Exam Prep series creates exams that will help you learn the subject matter as well as test you on your understanding. Each question is designed to help you master the concept. Just working through the exams, you gain an understanding of the subject--its a simple mechanical process that produces success.

INTEGRATED STUDY GUIDE AND REVIEW

MznLnx is not just a set of exams designed to test you, its also a comprehensive review of the subject content. Each exam question is also a review of the concept, making sure that you will get the answer correct without having to go to other sources of material. You learn as you go! Its the easiest way to pass an exam.

HUMOR

Studying can be tedious and dry. MznLnx's instructional design includes moderate humor within the exam questions on occassion, to break the tedium and revitalize the brain

Chapter 1. Introduction: The Role, History, and Direction of Management Accounting

1. _____ is concerned with the provisions and use of accounting information to managers within organizations, to provide them with the basis to make informed business decisions that will allow them to be better equipped in their management and control functions.

In contrast to financial accountancy information, _____ information is:

- usually confidential and used by management, instead of publicly reported;
- forward-looking, instead of historical;
- pragmatically computed using extensive management information systems and internal controls, instead of complying with accounting standards.

This is because of the different emphasis: _____ information is used within an organization, typically for decision-making.

a. Grenzplankostenrechnung
c. Nonassurance services
b. Governmental accounting
d. Management accounting

2. The _____ is a performance management tool which began as a concept for measuring whether the smaller-scale operational activities of a company are aligned with its larger-scale objectives in terms of vision and strategy.

By focusing not only on financial outcomes but also on the operational, marketing and developmental inputs to these, the _____ helps provide a more comprehensive view of a business, which in turn helps organizations act in their best long-term interests. This tool is also being used to address business response to climate change and greenhouse gas emissions.

a. Management by objectives
c. Best practice
b. Trustee
d. Balanced Scorecard

3. In economics, business, retail, and accounting, a _____ is the value of money that has been used up to produce something, and hence is not available for use anymore. In economics, a _____ is an alternative that is given up as a result of a decision. In business, the _____ may be one of acquisition, in which case the amount of money expended to acquire it is counted as _____.

a. Cost allocation
c. Cost of quality
b. Prime cost
d. Cost

4. An _____ is a practitioner of accountancy, which is the measurement, disclosure or provision of assurance about financial information that helps managers, investors, tax authorities and other decision makers make resource allocation decisions.

The word '_____' is derived from the French 'Compter' which took its origin from the Latin 'Computare'. The word was formerly written in English as 'Accomptant', but in process of time the word, which was always pronounced by dropping the 'p', became gradually changed both in pronunciation and in orthography to its present form.

Chapter 1. Introduction: The Role, History, and Direction of Management Accounting

a. ABC Television Network
b. AIG
c. AMEX
d. Accountant

5. The _____ is a professional organization headquartered in Montvale, New Jersey consisting of over 70,000 members worldwide. The IMA is dedicated to advancing the role of the management accountant and financial manager within the business organization, and provides relevant professional certification.

The IMA awards the Certified Management Accountant (CMA) designation in the United States.

a. International Accounting Standards Committee
b. Emerging technologies
c. Institute of Management Accountants
d. American Accounting Association

6. In financial accounting, a _____ is defined as an obligation of an entity arising from past transactions or events, the settlement of which may result in the transfer or use of assets, provision of services or other yielding of economic benefits in the future.
a. Vested
b. Corporate governance
c. False Claims Act
d. Liability

7. _____ Process Deming saw it as part of the 'system' whereby feedback from the process and customer were evaluated against organisational goals.
a. Procurement
b. Continuous improvement
c. Sole proprietorship
d. Sensitivity analysis

8. _____ is the process whereby companies use cost accounting to report or control the various costs of doing business.

The term _____ is widely used in business today. Unfortunately _____ has no uniform definition.

a. Process costing
b. Contribution margin analysis
c. Cost management
d. Contribution margin

9. _____ can be regarded as an outcome of mental processes (cognitive process) leading to the selection of a course of action among several alternatives. Every _____ process produces a final choice. The output can be an action or an opinion of choice.
a. 3M Company
b. BMC Software, Inc.
c. Decision making
d. BNSF Railway

10. Employment is a contract between two parties, one being the employer and the other being the _____. An _____ may be defined as: 'A person in the service of another under any contract of hire, express or implied, oral or written, where the employer has the power or right to control and direct the _____ in the material details of how the work is to be performed.' Black's Law Dictionary page 471 (5th ed. 1979.)
a. ABC Television Network
b. AIG
c. AMEX
d. Employee

11. _____ refers to increasing the spiritual, political, social or economic strength of individuals and communities. It often involves the empowered developing confidence in their own capacities.

Chapter 1. Introduction: The Role, History, and Direction of Management Accounting   3

The term Human _____ covers a vast landscape of meanings, interpretations, definitions and disciplines ranging from psychology and philosophy to the highly commercialized Self-Help industry and Motivational sciences.

a. IPO
b. Entity
c. IMF
d. Empowerment

12. _____ is systematic determination of merit, worth, and significance of something or someone using criteria against a set of standards. _____ often is used to characterize and appraise subjects of interest in a wide range of human enterprises, including the arts, criminal justice, foundations and non-profit organizations, government, health care, and other human services.

Depending on the topic of interest, there are professional groups which look to the quality and rigor of the _____ process.

a. AIG
b. AMEX
c. ABC Television Network
d. Evaluation

13. _____ is an acronym for First In, First Out, an abstraction in ways of organizing and manipulation of data relative to time and prioritization. This expression describes the principle of a queue processing technique or servicing conflicting demands by ordering process by first-come, first-served (FCFS) behaviour: what comes in first is handled first, what comes in next waits until the first is finished, etc.

Thus it is analogous to the behaviour of persons queueing (or 'standing in line', in common American parlance), where the persons leave the queue in the order they arrive, or waiting one's turn at a traffic control signal.

a. Kanban
b. Risk management
c. Trademark
d. FIFO

14. An _____ invented by esteemed professor Karen Osterheld is the system of records a business keeps to maintain its accounting system. This includes the purchase, sales, and other financial processes of the business. The purpose of an _____ is to accumulate data and provide decision makers (investors, creditors, and managers) with information to make decision While this was previously a paper-based process, most modern businesses now use accounting software such as UBS, MYOB etc.

a. AIG
b. ABC Television Network
c. AMEX
d. Accounting information system

15. _____ describes the situation when output from (or information about the result of) an event or phenomenon in the past will influence the same event/phenomenon in the present or future. When an event is part of a chain of cause-and-effect that forms a circuit or loop, then the event is said to 'feed back' into itself.

4 *Chapter 1. Introduction: The Role, History, and Direction of Management Accounting*

_____ is also a synonym for:

- _____ Signal; the information about the initial event that is the basis for subsequent modification of the event.
- _____ Loop; the causal path that leads from the initial generation of the _____ signal to the subsequent modification of the event.

_____ is a mechanism, process or signal that is looped back to control a system within itself. Such a loop is called a _____ loop.

a. Controllable
b. 3M Company
c. BMC Software, Inc.
d. Feedback

16. The _____ is a private, not-for-profit organization whose primary purpose is to develop generally accepted accounting principles (GAAP) within the United States in the public's interest. The Securities and Exchange Commission (SEC) designated the _____ as the organization responsible for setting accounting standards for public companies in the U.S. It was created in 1973, replacing the Accounting Principles Board and the Committee on Accounting Procedure of the American Institute of Certified Public Accountants. The _____'s mission is 'to establish and improve standards of financial accounting and reporting for the guidance and education of the public, including issuers, auditors, and users of financial information.'

The _____ is not a governmental body.

a. Governmental Accounting Standards Board
b. Fannie Mae
c. Financial Accounting Standards Board
d. Public company

17. The term _____ usually refers to a company that is permitted to offer its registered securities (stock, bonds, etc.) for sale to the general public, typically through a stock exchange, or occasionally a company whose stock is traded over the counter (OTC) via market makers who use non-exchange quotation services.

The term '_____' may also refer to a company owned by the government.

a. Public Company
b. Governmental Accounting Standards Board
c. Professional association
d. MicroStrategy

18. The _____ (sometimes called 'Peekaboo') is a private-sector, non-profit corporation created by the Sarbanes-Oxley Act, a 2002 United States federal law, to oversee the auditors of public companies. Its stated purpose is to 'protect the interests of investors and further the public interest in the preparation of informative, fair, and independent audit reports'. Although a private entity, the _____ has many government-like regulatory functions, making it in some ways similar to the private Self Regulatory Organizations (SROs) that regulate stock markets and other aspects of the financial markets in the United States.

a. 3M Company
b. Pension Benefit Guaranty Corporation
c. Financial Crimes Enforcement Network
d. Public Company Accounting Oversight Board

Chapter 1. Introduction: The Role, History, and Direction of Management Accounting

19. A _____ is a fungible, negotiable instrument representing financial value. they are broadly categorized into debt securities (such as banknotes, bonds and debentures), and equity securities; e.g., common stocks. The company or other entity issuing the _____ is called the issuer.
    a. Tracking stock
    b. BMC Software, Inc.
    c. 3M Company
    d. Security

20. The U.S. _____ is an independent agency of the United States government which holds primary responsibility for enforcing the federal securities laws and regulating the securities industry, the nation's stock and options exchanges, and other electronic securities markets. The SEC was created by section 4 of the Securities Exchange Act of 1934 (now codified as 15 U.S.C. ÂÂ§ 78d and commonly referred to as the 1934 Act.)
    a. BMC Software, Inc.
    b. BNSF Railway
    c. 3M Company
    d. Securities and Exchange Commission

21. An _____ is a term used in behavioral economics to describe those types of behaviors that impose costs on a person in the long-run that are not taken into account when making decisions in the present. Classical Economics discourages government from creating legislation that targets internalities, because it is assumed that the consumer takes these personal costs into account when paying for the good that causes the _____. For example, cigarettes should be taxed because of the negative consumption externalities that they impose, such as second-hand smoke, not because the smoker harms him or herself by smoking.
    a. Internality
    b. Operating budget
    c. Inventory turnover ratio
    d. Authorised capital

22. The _____ is the United States federal government agency that collects taxes and enforces the internal revenue laws. It is an agency within the U.S. Dept of the treasury responsible for interpretation and application of Federal tax law. The official U.S. Treasury regulations provide (in part):

    The _____ is a bureau of the Department of the Treasury under the immediate direction of the Commissioner of Internal Revenue.

    a. Indirect tax
    b. Use tax
    c. Internal Revenue Service
    d. Income tax

23. _____ is a method of identifying and evaluating activities that a business performs using activity-based costing to carry out a value chain analysis or a re-engineering initiative to improve strategic and operational decisions in an organization. Activity-based costing establishes relationships between overhead costs and activities so that overhead costs can be more precisely allocated to products, services, or customer segments. _____ focuses on managing activities to reduce costs and improve customer value.
    a. ABC Television Network
    b. Activity-based costing
    c. Indirect costs
    d. Activity-based management

24. A _____, also client, buyer or purchaser is the buyer or user of the paid products of an individual or organization, mostly called the supplier or seller. This is typically through purchasing or renting goods or services.

a. BMC Software, Inc.
b. Customer
c. BNSF Railway
d. 3M Company

25. The _____ is a concept from business management that was first described and popularized by Michael Porter in his 1985 best-seller, Competitive Advantage: Creating and Sustaining Superior Performance.

A _____ is a chain of activities. Products pass through all activities of the chain in order and at each activity the product gains some value.

a. Customer relationship management
b. Value chain
c. Product differentiation
d. Market segmentation

26. A '_____ is the system of organizations, people, technology, activities, information and resources involved in moving a product or service from supplier to customer. _____ activities transform natural resources, raw materials and components into a finished product that is delivered to the end customer. In sophisticated _____ systems, used products may re-enter the _____ at any point where residual value is recyclable.

a. Free port
b. Purchasing
c. Supply chain
d. Consignor

27. _____ is a business management strategy aimed at embedding awareness of quality in all organizational processes. _____ has been widely used in manufacturing, education, call centers, government, and service industries, as well as NASA space and science programs.

When used together as a phrase, the three words in this expression have the following meanings:

- Total: Involving the entire organization, supply chain, and/or product life cycle
- Quality: With its usual definitions, with all its complexities
- Management: The system of managing with steps like Plan, Organize, Control, Lead, Staff, provisioning and organizing.

As defined by the International Organization for Standardization (ISO):

'_____ is a management approach for an organization, centered on quality, based on the participation of all its members and aiming at long-term success through customer satisfaction, and benefits to all members of the organization and to society.' ISO 8402:1994

One major aim is to reduce variation from every process so that greater consistency of effort is obtained. (Royse, D., Thyer, B., Padgett D., ' Logan T., 2006)

Chapter 1. Introduction: The Role, History, and Direction of Management Accounting   7

In Japan, _____ comprises four process steps, namely:

1. Kaizen - Focuses on 'Continuous Process Improvement', to make processes visible, repeatable and measurable.
2. Atarimae Hinshitsu - The idea that 'things will work as they are supposed to'.
3. Kansei - Examining the way the user applies the product leads to improvement in the product itself.
4. Miryokuteki Hinshitsu - The idea that 'things should have an aesthetic quality' (for example, a pen will write in a way that is pleasing to the writer.)

_____ requires that the company maintain this quality standard in all aspects of its business. This requires ensuring that things are done right the first time and that defects and waste are eliminated from operations.

a. 3M Company
b. BNSF Railway
c. BMC Software, Inc.
d. Total quality management

28. The _____ of 2002 (Pub.L. 107-204, 116 Stat. 745, enacted July 30, 2002), also known as the Public Company Accounting Reform and Investor Protection Act of 2002, is a United States federal law enacted on July 30, 2002 in response to a number of major corporate and accounting scandals including those affecting Enron, Tyco International, Adelphia, Peregrine Systems and WorldCom. The legislation establishes new or enhanced standards for all U.S. public company boards, management, and public accounting firms. It does not apply to privately held companies.

a. Sarbanes-Oxley Act
b. FCPA
c. Fair Labor Standards Act
d. Lease

29. A _____ is the person responsible for running the treasury of an organization. In A new way to pay the National Debt (1786), James Gillray caricatured Queen Charlotte and George III awash with treasury funds to cover royal debts, with Pitt handing them another moneybag.

The Treasury of a country is the department responsible for the country's economy, finance and revenue. The _____ is generally the head of the Treasury, although, in some countries (such as the U.S. or the UK) the _____ reports to a Secretary of the Treasury, or Chancellor of the Exchequer.

a. 3M Company
b. Treasurer
c. BNSF Railway
d. BMC Software, Inc.

30. _____ is the study of how the variation (uncertainty) in the output of a mathematical model can be apportioned, qualitatively or quantitatively, to different sources of variation in the input of a model.

In more general terms uncertainty and sensitivity analyses investigate the robustness of a study when the study includes some form of mathematical modelling. While uncertainty analysis studies the overall uncertainty in the conclusions of the study, _____ tries to identify what source of uncertainty weights more on the study's conclusions.

8 *Chapter 1. Introduction: The Role, History, and Direction of Management Accounting*

    a. Kaizen
    b. Time to market
    c. Free cash flow
    d. Sensitivity analysis

31. The general definition of an _____ is an evaluation of a person, organization, system, process, project or product. _____s are performed to ascertain the validity and reliability of information; also to provide an assessment of a system's internal control. The goal of an _____ is to express an opinion on the person/organization/system (etc) in question, under evaluation based on work done on a test basis.
    a. Assurance service
    b. Institute of Chartered Accountants of India
    c. Audit regime
    d. Audit

32. _____ refers to the confirmation of certain characteristics of an object, person, or organization. This confirmation is often, but not always, provided by some form of external review, education, or assessment. One of the most common types of _____ in modern society is professional _____, where a person is certified as being able to competently complete a job or task, usually by the passing of an examination.
    a. BNSF Railway
    b. Certification
    c. 3M Company
    d. BMC Software, Inc.

33. The title _____ is a professional designation awarded by various professional bodies around the world.

The _____ designation is a post-nominal award issued to individuals who have achieved a peer-based criteria of professional competency in the field of Management Accounting. Management accounting qualifications differ from those such as the ACA or CPA 'Chartered' or 'Public' accounting qualifications in a number of ways.

    a. Convey Compliance Systems
    b. 3M Company
    c. BMC Software, Inc.
    d. Certified management accountant

34. _____ is the statutory title of qualified accountants in the United States who have passed the Uniform _____ Examination and have met additional state education and experience requirements for certification as a _____. Individuals who have passed the Exam but have not either accomplished the required on-the-job experience or have previously met it but in the meantime have lapsed their continuing professional education are, in many states, permitted the designation '_____ Inactive' or an equivalent phrase. In most U.S. states, only _____s who are licensed are able to provide to the public attestation (including auditing) opinions on financial statements.
    a. Certified General Accountant
    b. Chartered Certified Accountant
    c. Chartered Accountant
    d. Certified public accountant

35. _____ is a profession and activity involved in helping organisations achieve their stated objectives. It does this by using a systematic methodology for analyzing business processes, procedures and activities with the goal of highlighting organizational problems and recommending solutions. Professionals called internal auditors are employed by organizations to perform the _____ activity.
    a. ITGCs
    b. Information audit
    c. Assurance service
    d. Internal auditing

36. Internal auditing is a profession and activity involved in helping organisations achieve their stated objectives. It does this by utilizing a systematic methodology for analyzing business processes, procedures and activities with the goal of highlighting organizational problems and recommending solutions. Professionals called _____ are employed by organizations to perform the internal auditing activity.

a. Auditor independence
c. Auditing Standards Board
b. Internal auditors
d. Internal Auditing

Chapter 2. Basic Management Accounting Concepts

1. _____ is concerned with the provisions and use of accounting information to managers within organizations, to provide them with the basis to make informed business decisions that will allow them to be better equipped in their management and control functions.

In contrast to financial accountancy information, _____ information is:

- usually confidential and used by management, instead of publicly reported;
- forward-looking, instead of historical;
- pragmatically computed using extensive management information systems and internal controls, instead of complying with accounting standards.

This is because of the different emphasis: _____ information is used within an organization, typically for decision-making.

a. Governmental accounting
b. Grenzplankostenrechnung
c. Nonassurance services
d. Management accounting

2. In financial accounting, a _____ is defined as an obligation of an entity arising from past transactions or events, the settlement of which may result in the transfer or use of assets, provision of services or other yielding of economic benefits in the future.
a. Corporate governance
b. Vested
c. Liability
d. False Claims Act

3. In economics, business, retail, and accounting, a _____ is the value of money that has been used up to produce something, and hence is not available for use anymore. In economics, a _____ is an alternative that is given up as a result of a decision. In business, the _____ may be one of acquisition, in which case the amount of money expended to acquire it is counted as _____.
a. Cost
b. Prime cost
c. Cost allocation
d. Cost of quality

4. _____ is a process of attributing cost to particular cost centres. For example the wage of the driver of the purchasing department can be allocated to the purchasing department cost centre. It is not necessary to share the wage cost over several different cost centers.
a. Cost of quality
b. Variable cost
c. Cost allocation
d. Cost accounting

5. A _____ is a tangible input for a product manufactured/Service provided, like labor or material. For example a cloth manufacturing firm requires some amount of predetermined labor and predetermined raw material for any amount of cloth being manufactured. The cost of employing labor can be directly fixed as 'per man per hour' or 'per man per day', so the labor is a _____ as you can directly associate cost with it.
a. 3M Company
b. Residual value
c. Cost object
d. Round-tripping

6. In accounting, _____ has a very specific meaning. It is an outflow of cash or other valuable assets from a person or company to another person or company. This outflow of cash is generally one side of a trade for products or services that have equal or better current or future value to the buyer than to the seller.

Chapter 2. Basic Management Accounting Concepts

a. AMEX
b. ABC Television Network
c. AIG
d. Expense

7. _____ or economic opportunity loss is the value of the next best alternative foregone as the result of making a decision. _____ analysis is an important part of a company's decision-making processes but is not treated as an actual cost in any financial statement. The next best thing that a person can engage in is referred to as the _____ of doing the best thing and ignoring the next best thing to be done.
   a. ABC Television Network
   b. AIG
   c. Opportunity cost
   d. Inflation

8. _____s are expenses that change in proportion to the activity of a business. In other words, _____ is the sum of marginal costs. It can also be considered normal costs.
   a. Variable cost
   b. Quality costs
   c. Fixed costs
   d. Cost accounting

9. _____ are costs that are not directly accountable to a particular function or product. _____ may be either fixed or variable. _____ include taxes, administration, personnel and security costs, and are also known as overhead.
   a. Activity-based costing
   b. Activity-based management
   c. ABC Television Network
   d. Indirect costs

10. _____ is an acronym for First In, First Out, an abstraction in ways of organizing and manipulation of data relative to time and prioritization. This expression describes the principle of a queue processing technique or servicing conflicting demands by ordering process by first-come, first-served (FCFS) behaviour: what comes in first is handled first, what comes in next waits until the first is finished, etc.

Thus it is analogous to the behaviour of persons queueing (or 'standing in line', in common American parlance), where the persons leave the queue in the order they arrive, or waiting one's turn at a traffic control signal.

   a. FIFO
   b. Kanban
   c. Risk management
   d. Trademark

11. A _____ is a fungible, negotiable instrument representing financial value. they are broadly categorized into debt securities (such as banknotes, bonds and debentures), and equity securities; e.g., common stocks. The company or other entity issuing the _____ is called the issuer.
   a. Tracking stock
   b. 3M Company
   c. BMC Software, Inc.
   d. Security

12. The U.S. _____ is an independent agency of the United States government which holds primary responsibility for enforcing the federal securities laws and regulating the securities industry, the nation's stock and options exchanges, and other electronic securities markets. The SEC was created by section 4 of the Securities Exchange Act of 1934 (now codified as 15 U.S.C. §§ 78d and commonly referred to as the 1934 Act.)
   a. BNSF Railway
   b. Securities and Exchange Commission
   c. 3M Company
   d. BMC Software, Inc.

13. In law, tangibility is the attribute of being detectable with the senses.

Chapter 2. Basic Management Accounting Concepts

In criminal law, one of the elements of an offense of larceny is that the stolen property must be _____.

In the context of intellectual property, expression in _____ form is one of the requirements for copyright protection.

a. Nonacquiescence
b. Headnote
c. Contingent liabilities
d. Tangible

14. An _____ is a practitioner of accountancy, which is the measurement, disclosure or provision of assurance about financial information that helps managers, investors, tax authorities and other decision makers make resource allocation decisions.

The word '_____' is derived from the French 'Compter' which took its origin from the Latin 'Computare'. The word was formerly written in English as 'Accomptant', but in process of time the word, which was always pronounced by dropping the 'p', became gradually changed both in pronunciation and in orthography to its present form.

a. Accountant
b. AIG
c. ABC Television Network
d. AMEX

15. The _____ is a performance management tool which began as a concept for measuring whether the smaller-scale operational activities of a company are aligned with its larger-scale objectives in terms of vision and strategy.

By focusing not only on financial outcomes but also on the operational, marketing and developmental inputs to these, the _____ helps provide a more comprehensive view of a business, which in turn helps organizations act in their best long-term interests. This tool is also being used to address business response to climate change and greenhouse gas emissions.

a. Management by objectives
b. Best practice
c. Balanced Scorecard
d. Trustee

16. The _____ is a professional organization headquartered in Montvale, New Jersey consisting of over 70,000 members worldwide. The IMA is dedicated to advancing the role of the management accountant and financial manager within the business organization, and provides relevant professional certification.

The IMA awards the Certified Management Accountant (CMA) designation in the United States.

a. International Accounting Standards Committee
b. American Accounting Association
c. Emerging technologies
d. Institute of Management Accountants

Chapter 2. Basic Management Accounting Concepts 13

17. An _____ is a term used in behavioral economics to describe those types of behaviors that impose costs on a person in the long-run that are not taken into account when making decisions in the present. Classical Economics discourages government from creating legislation that targets internalities, because it is assumed that the consumer takes these personal costs into account when paying for the good that causes the _____. For example, cigarettes should be taxed because of the negative consumption externalities that they impose, such as second-hand smoke, not because the smoker harms him or herself by smoking.

 a. Inventory turnover ratio
 b. Internality
 c. Operating budget
 d. Authorised capital

18. The _____ is the United States federal government agency that collects taxes and enforces the internal revenue laws. It is an agency within the U.S. Dept of the treasury responsible for interpretation and application of Federal tax law. The official U.S. Treasury regulations provide (in part):

The _____ is a bureau of the Department of the Treasury under the immediate direction of the Commissioner of Internal Revenue.

 a. Indirect tax
 b. Income tax
 c. Use tax
 d. Internal Revenue Service

19. The _____ is a concept from business management that was first described and popularized by Michael Porter in his 1985 best-seller, Competitive Advantage: Creating and Sustaining Superior Performance.

A _____ is a chain of activities. Products pass through all activities of the chain in order and at each activity the product gains some value.

 a. Value chain
 b. Market segmentation
 c. Customer relationship management
 d. Product differentiation

20. A _____ is an entity formed between two or more parties to undertake economic activity together. The parties agree to create a new entity by both contributing equity, and they then share in the revenues, expenses, and control of the enterprise. The venture can be for one specific project only, or a continuing business relationship such as the Fuji Xerox _____.

 a. Chief Financial Officers Act of 1990
 b. Joint venture
 c. Pre-emption right
 d. Fraud Enforcement and Recovery Act

21. _____ is an accounting methodology that traces and accumulates direct costs, and allocates indirect costs of a manufacturing process. Costs are assigned to products, usually in a large batch, which might include an entire month's production. Eventually, costs have to be allocated to individual units of product.

 a. Cost driver
 b. Profit center
 c. Process costing
 d. Cost management

22. In business, _____, Overhead cost or _____ expense refers to an ongoing expense of operating a business. The term _____ is usually used to group expenses that are necessary to the continued functioning of the business, but do not directly generate profits.

_____ expenses are all costs on the income statement except for direct labor and direct materials.

a. Intangible assets
b. ABC Television Network
c. AIG
d. Overhead

23. Direct labor and overhead are often called conversion cost while direct material and direct labor are often referred to as _____.

For example, a manufacturing firm pays for raw materials. When activity is decreased, less raw material is used, and so the spending for raw materials falls.

a. Prime cost
b. Cost-volume-profit analysis
c. Cost accounting
d. Marginal cost

24. Total _____ is a method of Accounting cost which entails the full cost of manufacturing or providing a service. This includes not just the costs of materials and labour, but also of all manufacturing overheads (whether e;fixede; or e;variablee;.) One of the main reasons for absorbing overheads into the cost of units is for inventory valuation purposes.

a. Absorption costing
b. AMEX
c. ABC Television Network
d. AIG

25. In financial accounting, _____ or cost of sales includes the direct costs attributable to the production of the goods sold by a company. This amount includes the materials cost used in creating the goods along with the direct labor costs used to produce the good. It excludes indirect expenses such as distribution costs and sales force costs.

a. Reorder point
b. 3M Company
c. FIFO and LIFO accounting
d. Cost of goods sold

26. _____ are formal records of a business' financial activities.

In British English, including United Kingdom company law, _____ are often referred to as accounts, although the term _____ is also used, particularly by accountants.

_____ provide an overview of a business' financial condition in both short and long term.

a. Notes to the financial statements
b. Statement of retained earnings
c. 3M Company
d. Financial statements

27. _____ is a company's financial statement that indicates how the revenue is transformed into the net income The purpose of the _____ is to show managers and investors whether the company made or lost money during the period being reported.

The important thing to remember about an _____ is that it represents a period of time.

a. Income statement
b. AIG
c. ABC Television Network
d. AMEX

Chapter 2. Basic Management Accounting Concepts

28. _____ is the practical application of management techniques to control and report on the financial health of the organization. This involves the analysis, planning, implementation, and control of programs designed to provide financial data reporting for managerial decision making. This includes the maintenance of bank accounts, developing financial statements, cash flow and financial performance analysis.
   a. Activity-based costing
   b. Activity-based management
   c. ABC Television Network
   d. Accounting management

29. _____ is a method of identifying and evaluating activities that a business performs using activity-based costing to carry out a value chain analysis or a re-engineering initiative to improve strategic and operational decisions in an organization. Activity-based costing establishes relationships between overhead costs and activities so that overhead costs can be more precisely allocated to products, services, or customer segments. _____ focuses on managing activities to reduce costs and improve customer value.
   a. ABC Television Network
   b. Indirect costs
   c. Activity-based costing
   d. Activity-based Management

30. _____ is a costing model that identifies activities in an organization and assigns the cost of each activity resource to all products and services according to the actual consumption by each: it assigns more indirect costs (overhead) into direct costs.

In this way an organization can establish the true cost of its individual products and services for the purposes of identifying and eliminating those which are unprofitable and lowering the prices of those which are overpriced.

In a business organization, the ABC methodology assigns an organization's resource costs through activities to the products and services provided to its customers.

   a. Activity-based costing
   b. Indirect costs
   c. Activity-based management
   d. ABC Television Network

31. _____ is a demonstration of a process -- such as a variable, term, or object -- relative in terms of the specific process or set of validation tests used to determine its presence and quantity. Properties described in this manner must be sufficiently accessible, so that persons other than the definer may independently measure or test for them at will. An _____ is generally designed to model a conceptual definition.
   a. ABC Television Network
   b. AMEX
   c. Operational definition
   d. AIG

Chapter 3. Activity Cost Behavior

1. In economics, business, retail, and accounting, a _____ is the value of money that has been used up to produce something, and hence is not available for use anymore. In economics, a _____ is an alternative that is given up as a result of a decision. In business, the _____ may be one of acquisition, in which case the amount of money expended to acquire it is counted as _____.
   a. Cost
   b. Prime cost
   c. Cost allocation
   d. Cost of quality

2. The _____ is a private, not-for-profit organization whose primary purpose is to develop generally accepted accounting principles (GAAP) within the United States in the public's interest. The Securities and Exchange Commission (SEC) designated the _____ as the organization responsible for setting accounting standards for public companies in the U.S. It was created in 1973, replacing the Accounting Principles Board and the Committee on Accounting Procedure of the American Institute of Certified Public Accountants. The _____'s mission is 'to establish and improve standards of financial accounting and reporting for the guidance and education of the public, including issuers, auditors, and users of financial information.'

   The _____ is not a governmental body.

   a. Governmental Accounting Standards Board
   b. Public company
   c. Fannie Mae
   d. Financial Accounting Standards Board

3. In economics, _____ are business expenses that are not dependent on the activities of the business They tend to be time-related, such as salaries or rents being paid per month. This is in contrast to variable costs, which are volume-related (and are paid per quantity.)

   In management accounting, _____ are defined as expenses that do not change in proportion to the activity of a business, within the relevant period or scale of production.

   a. Cost accounting
   b. Cost of quality
   c. Marginal cost
   d. Fixed costs

4. _____ is an acronym for First In, First Out, an abstraction in ways of organizing and manipulation of data relative to time and prioritization. This expression describes the principle of a queue processing technique or servicing conflicting demands by ordering process by first-come, first-served (FCFS) behaviour: what comes in first is handled first, what comes in next waits until the first is finished, etc.

   Thus it is analogous to the behaviour of persons queueing (or 'standing in line', in common American parlance), where the persons leave the queue in the order they arrive, or waiting one's turn at a traffic control signal.

   a. Kanban
   b. Trademark
   c. Risk management
   d. FIFO

5. _____s are expenses that change in proportion to the activity of a business. In other words, _____ is the sum of marginal costs. It can also be considered normal costs.
   a. Cost accounting
   b. Variable cost
   c. Fixed costs
   d. Quality costs

Chapter 3. Activity Cost Behavior

6. A _____ is an entity formed between two or more parties to undertake economic activity together. The parties agree to create a new entity by both contributing equity, and they then share in the revenues, expenses, and control of the enterprise. The venture can be for one specific project only, or a continuing business relationship such as the Fuji Xerox _____.

a. Pre-emption right
b. Fraud Enforcement and Recovery Act
c. Chief Financial Officers Act of 1990
d. Joint venture

7. The _____ is a performance management tool which began as a concept for measuring whether the smaller-scale operational activities of a company are aligned with its larger-scale objectives in terms of vision and strategy.

By focusing not only on financial outcomes but also on the operational, marketing and developmental inputs to these, the _____ helps provide a more comprehensive view of a business, which in turn helps organizations act in their best long-term interests. This tool is also being used to address business response to climate change and greenhouse gas emissions.

a. Trustee
b. Best practice
c. Balanced Scorecard
d. Management by objectives

8. An _____ is a practitioner of accountancy, which is the measurement, disclosure or provision of assurance about financial information that helps managers, investors, tax authorities and other decision makers make resource allocation decisions.

The word '_____' is derived from the French 'Compter' which took its origin from the Latin 'Computare'. The word was formerly written in English as 'Accomptant', but in process of time the word, which was always pronounced by dropping the 'p', became gradually changed both in pronunciation and in orthography to its present form.

a. AMEX
b. ABC Television Network
c. Accountant
d. AIG

9. The _____ is a professional organization headquartered in Montvale, New Jersey consisting of over 70,000 members worldwide. The IMA is dedicated to advancing the role of the management accountant and financial manager within the business organization, and provides relevant professional certification.

The IMA awards the Certified Management Accountant (CMA) designation in the United States.

a. Emerging technologies
b. American Accounting Association
c. International Accounting Standards Committee
d. Institute of Management Accountants

10. _____ is concerned with the provisions and use of accounting information to managers within organizations, to provide them with the basis to make informed business decisions that will allow them to be better equipped in their management and control functions.

Chapter 3. Activity Cost Behavior

In contrast to financial accountancy information, _____ information is:

- usually confidential and used by management, instead of publicly reported;
- forward-looking, instead of historical;
- pragmatically computed using extensive management information systems and internal controls, instead of complying with accounting standards.

This is because of the different emphasis: _____ information is used within an organization, typically for decision-making.

a. Nonassurance services
c. Governmental accounting
b. Grenzplankostenrechnung
d. Management accounting

11. _____ is accounting for the lean enterprise. It seeks to move from traditional cost accounting to a system that measures and motivates good business practices in the lean enterprise.

Lean manufacturing methods were first introduced into the United States and other Western countries in the 1980's; primarily by the Toyota companies.

a. BMC Software, Inc.
c. BNSF Railway
b. Lean accounting
d. 3M Company

12. In financial accounting, a _____ is defined as an obligation of an entity arising from past transactions or events, the settlement of which may result in the transfer or use of assets, provision of services or other yielding of economic benefits in the future.

a. False Claims Act
c. Vested
b. Liability
d. Corporate governance

13. The terms '_____' and 'independent variable' are used in similar but subtly different ways in mathematics and statistics as part of the standard terminology in those subjects. They are used to distinguish between two types of quantities being considered, separating them into those available at the start of a process and those being created by it, where the latter (_____s) are dependent on the former (independent variables.)

In traditional calculus, a function is defined as a relation between two terms called variables because their values vary.

a. Dependent variable
c. BMC Software, Inc.
b. BNSF Railway
d. 3M Company

14. The terms 'dependent variable' and '_____' are used in similar but subtly different ways in mathematics and statistics as part of the standard terminology in those subjects. They are used to distinguish between two types of quantities being considered, separating them into those available at the start of a process and those being created by it, where the latter (dependent variables) are dependent on the former (_____s.)

Chapter 3. Activity Cost Behavior

In traditional calculus, a function is defined as a relation between two terms called variables because their values vary.

a. ABC Television Network
b. AMEX
c. AIG
d. Independent variable

15. The _____ of 2002 (Pub.L. 107-204, 116 Stat. 745, enacted July 30, 2002), also known as the Public Company Accounting Reform and Investor Protection Act of 2002, is a United States federal law enacted on July 30, 2002 in response to a number of major corporate and accounting scandals including those affecting Enron, Tyco International, Adelphia, Peregrine Systems and WorldCom. The legislation establishes new or enhanced standards for all U.S. public company boards, management, and public accounting firms. It does not apply to privately held companies.

a. Lease
b. Fair Labor Standards Act
c. Sarbanes-Oxley Act
d. FCPA

16. In statistics, _____ refers to techniques for the modeling and analysis of numerical data consisting of values of a dependent variable and of one or more independent variables The dependent variable in the regression equation is modeled as a function of the independent variables, corresponding parameters, and an error term. The error term is treated as a random variable.

a. 3M Company
b. Multicollinearity
c. Trend analysis
d. Regression analysis

17. A _____ is a computer application that simulates a paper worksheet. It displays multiple cells that together make up a grid consisting of rows and columns, each cell containing either alphanumeric text or numeric values. A _____ cell may alternatively contain a formula that defines how the contents of that cell is to be calculated from the contents of any other cell (or combination of cells) each time any cell is updated.

a. Linear regression
b. Merck ' Co., Inc.
c. Mutual fund
d. Spreadsheet

18. _____ is the term used to refer to the standard framework of guidelines for financial accounting used in any given jurisdiction. _____ includes the standards, conventions, and rules accountants follow in recording and summarizing transactions, and in the preparation of financial statements.

Financial accounting information must be assembled and reported objectively.

a. Current asset
b. Long-term liabilities
c. Generally Accepted Accounting Principles
d. General ledger

19. In statistics, the _____, R^2 is used in the context of statistical models whose main purpose is the prediction of future outcomes on the basis of other related information. It is the proportion of variability in a data set that is accounted for by the statistical model. It provides a measure of how well future outcomes are likely to be predicted by the model.

a. Regression analysis
b. Trend analysis
c. 3M Company
d. Coefficient of determination

20. The _____ of a statistical model describes how well it fits a set of observations. Measures of _____ typically summarize the discrepancy between observed values and the values expected under the model in question. Such measures can be used in statistical hypothesis testing, e.g. to test for normality of residuals, to test whether two samples are drawn from identical distributions , or whether outcome frequencies follow a specified distribution
   a. BNSF Railway
   b. BMC Software, Inc.
   c. 3M Company
   d. Goodness of fit

Chapter 4. Activity-Based Product Costing   21

1. The _____ is a performance management tool which began as a concept for measuring whether the smaller-scale operational activities of a company are aligned with its larger-scale objectives in terms of vision and strategy.

By focusing not only on financial outcomes but also on the operational, marketing and developmental inputs to these, the _____ helps provide a more comprehensive view of a business, which in turn helps organizations act in their best long-term interests. This tool is also being used to address business response to climate change and greenhouse gas emissions.

   a. Best practice
   c. Trustee
   b. Management by objectives
   d. Balanced Scorecard

2. In financial accounting, a _____ is defined as an obligation of an entity arising from past transactions or events, the settlement of which may result in the transfer or use of assets, provision of services or other yielding of economic benefits in the future.
   a. Vested
   c. Liability
   b. False Claims Act
   d. Corporate governance

3. In economics, business, retail, and accounting, a _____ is the value of money that has been used up to produce something, and hence is not available for use anymore. In economics, a _____ is an alternative that is given up as a result of a decision. In business, the _____ may be one of acquisition, in which case the amount of money expended to acquire it is counted as _____.
   a. Prime cost
   c. Cost allocation
   b. Cost
   d. Cost of quality

4. _____ is a process of attributing cost to particular cost centres. For example the wage of the driver of the purchasing department can be allocated to the purchasing department cost centre. It is not necessary to share the wage cost over several different cost centers.
   a. Cost accounting
   c. Variable cost
   b. Cost of quality
   d. Cost allocation

5. _____ is an acronym for First In, First Out, an abstraction in ways of organizing and manipulation of data relative to time and prioritization. This expression describes the principle of a queue processing technique or servicing conflicting demands by ordering process by first-come, first-served (FCFS) behaviour: what comes in first is handled first, what comes in next waits until the first is finished, etc.

Thus it is analogous to the behaviour of persons queueing (or 'standing in line', in common American parlance), where the persons leave the queue in the order they arrive, or waiting one's turn at a traffic control signal.

   a. Trademark
   c. Risk management
   b. Kanban
   d. FIFO

6. A _____ is an entity formed between two or more parties to undertake economic activity together. The parties agree to create a new entity by both contributing equity, and they then share in the revenues, expenses, and control of the enterprise. The venture can be for one specific project only, or a continuing business relationship such as the Fuji Xerox _____.

a. Pre-emption right
b. Fraud Enforcement and Recovery Act
c. Joint venture
d. Chief Financial Officers Act of 1990

7. In business, _____, Overhead cost or _____ expense refers to an ongoing expense of operating a business. The term _____ is usually used to group expenses that are necessary to the continued functioning of the business, but do not directly generate profits.

_____ expenses are all costs on the income statement except for direct labor and direct materials.

a. ABC Television Network
b. Overhead
c. AIG
d. Intangible assets

8. A _____ is the rate used to apply manufacturing overhead to work-in-process inventory. It is calculated as estimated manufacturing overhead cost divided by estimated amount of cost driver or activity base. Common activity bases used in the calculation include direct labor costs, direct labor hours, or machine hours.

a. Sensitivity analysis
b. Kaizen
c. Pre-determined overhead rate
d. Procurement

9. In probability theory and statistics, the _____ of a random variable, probability distribution averaging the squared distance of its possible values from the expected value (mean.) Whereas the mean is a way to describe the location of a distribution, the _____ is a way to capture its scale or degree of being spread out. The unit of _____ is the square of the unit of the original variable.

a. Statistics
b. Monte Carlo methods
c. Time series
d. Variance

10. In management accounting, _____ establishes budget and actual cost of operations, processes, departments or product and the analysis of variances, profitability or social use of funds. Managers use _____ to support decision-making to cut a company's costs and improve profitability. As a form of management accounting, _____ need not follow standards such as GAAP, because its primary use is for internal managers, rather than outside users, and what to compute is instead decided pragmatically.

a. Cost-volume-profit analysis
b. Prime cost
c. Marginal cost
d. Cost accounting

11. _____ is a common concept in economics, and gives rise to derived concepts such as consumer debt. Generally _____ is defined by opposition to production. But the precise definition can vary because different schools of economists define production quite differently.

a. Consumption
b. Starving the beast
c. Yield
d. Mitigating Control

12. _____ is a costing model that identifies activities in an organization and assigns the cost of each activity resource to all products and services according to the actual consumption by each: it assigns more indirect costs (overhead) into direct costs.

In this way an organization can establish the true cost of its individual products and services for the purposes of identifying and eliminating those which are unprofitable and lowering the prices of those which are overpriced.

Chapter 4. Activity-Based Product Costing

In a business organization, the ABC methodology assigns an organization's resource costs through activities to the products and services provided to its customers.

a. ABC Television Network
b. Activity-based management
c. Indirect costs
d. Activity-based costing

13. The _____ of 2002 (Pub.L. 107-204, 116 Stat. 745, enacted July 30, 2002), also known as the Public Company Accounting Reform and Investor Protection Act of 2002, is a United States federal law enacted on July 30, 2002 in response to a number of major corporate and accounting scandals including those affecting Enron, Tyco International, Adelphia, Peregrine Systems and WorldCom. The legislation establishes new or enhanced standards for all U.S. public company boards, management, and public accounting firms. It does not apply to privately held companies.

a. FCPA
b. Lease
c. Fair Labor Standards Act
d. Sarbanes-Oxley Act

14. An _____ is a practitioner of accountancy, which is the measurement, disclosure or provision of assurance about financial information that helps managers, investors, tax authorities and other decision makers make resource allocation decisions.

The word '_____' is derived from the French 'Compter' which took its origin from the Latin 'Computare'. The word was formerly written in English as 'Accomptant', but in process of time the word, which was always pronounced by dropping the 'p', became gradually changed both in pronunciation and in orthography to its present form.

a. Accountant
b. AIG
c. ABC Television Network
d. AMEX

15. The _____ is a professional organization headquartered in Montvale, New Jersey consisting of over 70,000 members worldwide. The IMA is dedicated to advancing the role of the management accountant and financial manager within the business organization, and provides relevant professional certification.

The IMA awards the Certified Management Accountant (CMA) designation in the United States.

a. American Accounting Association
b. Emerging technologies
c. International Accounting Standards Committee
d. Institute of Management Accountants

16. _____ is concerned with the provisions and use of accounting information to managers within organizations, to provide them with the basis to make informed business decisions that will allow them to be better equipped in their management and control functions.

In contrast to financial accountancy information, _____ information is:

- usually confidential and used by management, instead of publicly reported;
- forward-looking, instead of historical;
- pragmatically computed using extensive management information systems and internal controls, instead of complying with accounting standards.

This is because of the different emphasis: _____ information is used within an organization, typically for decision-making.

a. Grenzplankostenrechnung
b. Nonassurance services
c. Governmental accounting
d. Management accounting

17. A _____ is a fungible, negotiable instrument representing financial value. they are broadly categorized into debt securities (such as banknotes, bonds and debentures), and equity securities; e.g., common stocks. The company or other entity issuing the _____ is called the issuer.
a. BMC Software, Inc.
b. Tracking stock
c. Security
d. 3M Company

18. The U.S. _____ is an independent agency of the United States government which holds primary responsibility for enforcing the federal securities laws and regulating the securities industry, the nation's stock and options exchanges, and other electronic securities markets. The SEC was created by section 4 of the Securities Exchange Act of 1934 (now codified as 15 U.S.C. ÂÂ§ 78d and commonly referred to as the 1934 Act.)
a. BNSF Railway
b. 3M Company
c. BMC Software, Inc.
d. Securities and Exchange Commission

Chapter 5. Activity-Based Management

1. _____ is a method of identifying and evaluating activities that a business performs using activity-based costing to carry out a value chain analysis or a re-engineering initiative to improve strategic and operational decisions in an organization. Activity-based costing establishes relationships between overhead costs and activities so that overhead costs can be more precisely allocated to products, services, or customer segments. _____ focuses on managing activities to reduce costs and improve customer value.
    a. ABC Television Network
    b. Indirect costs
    c. Activity-based costing
    d. Activity-based management

2. The _____ is a performance management tool which began as a concept for measuring whether the smaller-scale operational activities of a company are aligned with its larger-scale objectives in terms of vision and strategy.

    By focusing not only on financial outcomes but also on the operational, marketing and developmental inputs to these, the _____ helps provide a more comprehensive view of a business, which in turn helps organizations act in their best long-term interests. This tool is also being used to address business response to climate change and greenhouse gas emissions.

    a. Balanced Scorecard
    b. Trustee
    c. Best practice
    d. Management by objectives

3. _____ is an accounting methodology that traces and accumulates direct costs, and allocates indirect costs of a manufacturing process. Costs are assigned to products, usually in a large batch, which might include an entire month's production. Eventually, costs have to be allocated to individual units of product.
    a. Cost management
    b. Profit center
    c. Cost driver
    d. Process costing

4. The _____ is a private, not-for-profit organization whose primary purpose is to develop generally accepted accounting principles (GAAP) within the United States in the public's interest. The Securities and Exchange Commission (SEC) designated the _____ as the organization responsible for setting accounting standards for public companies in the U.S. It was created in 1973, replacing the Accounting Principles Board and the Committee on Accounting Procedure of the American Institute of Certified Public Accountants. The _____'s mission is 'to establish and improve standards of financial accounting and reporting for the guidance and education of the public, including issuers, auditors, and users of financial information.'

    The _____ is not a governmental body.

    a. Public company
    b. Fannie Mae
    c. Financial Accounting Standards Board
    d. Governmental Accounting Standards Board

5. _____ is systematic determination of merit, worth, and significance of something or someone using criteria against a set of standards. _____ often is used to characterize and appraise subjects of interest in a wide range of human enterprises, including the arts, criminal justice, foundations and non-profit organizations, government, health care, and other human services.

    Depending on the topic of interest, there are professional groups which look to the quality and rigor of the _____ process.

a. AIG
b. ABC Television Network
c. AMEX
d. Evaluation

6. _____ is an acronym for First In, First Out, an abstraction in ways of organizing and manipulation of data relative to time and prioritization. This expression describes the principle of a queue processing technique or servicing conflicting demands by ordering process by first-come, first-served (FCFS) behaviour: what comes in first is handled first, what comes in next waits until the first is finished, etc.

Thus it is analogous to the behaviour of persons queueing (or 'standing in line', in common American parlance), where the persons leave the queue in the order they arrive, or waiting one's turn at a traffic control signal.

a. Kanban
b. Trademark
c. FIFO
d. Risk management

7. In economics, business, retail, and accounting, a _____ is the value of money that has been used up to produce something, and hence is not available for use anymore. In economics, a _____ is an alternative that is given up as a result of a decision. In business, the _____ may be one of acquisition, in which case the amount of money expended to acquire it is counted as _____.

a. Cost of quality
b. Prime cost
c. Cost allocation
d. Cost

8. A _____ is an entity formed between two or more parties to undertake economic activity together. The parties agree to create a new entity by both contributing equity, and they then share in the revenues, expenses, and control of the enterprise. The venture can be for one specific project only, or a continuing business relationship such as the Fuji Xerox _____.

a. Fraud Enforcement and Recovery Act
b. Pre-emption right
c. Chief Financial Officers Act of 1990
d. Joint venture

9. _____ refers to the additional value of a commodity over the cost of commodities used to produce it from the previous stage of production. An example is the price of gasoline at the pump over the price of the oil in it. In national accounts used in macroeconomics, it refers to the contribution of the factors of production, i.e., land, labor, and capital goods, to raising the value of a product and corresponds to the incomes received by the owners of these factors.

a. Supply-side economics
b. Value added
c. 3M Company
d. Minimum wage

10. _____ is a Japanese philosophy that focuses on continuous improvement throughout all aspects of life. When applied to the workplace, _____ activities continually improve all functions of a business, from manufacturing to management and from the CEO to the assembly line workers. By improving standardized activities and processes, _____ aims to eliminate waste .

a. Kaizen
b. Sensitivity analysis
c. Proprietorship
d. Procurement

Chapter 5. Activity-Based Management

11. _____ refers to a business or organization attempting to acquire goods or services to accomplish the goals of the enterprise. Though there are several organizations that attempt to set standards in the _____ process, processes can vary greatly between organizations. Typically the word e;_____e; is not used interchangeably with the word e;procuremente;, since procurement typically includes Expediting, Supplier Quality, and Traffic and Logistics (T'L) in addition to _____.
   a. Consignor
   b. Supply chain
   c. Purchasing
   d. Free port

12. The term '_____' refers to the concept of collecting information and attempting to spot a pattern in the information. In some fields of study, the term '_____' has more formally-defined meanings.

In project management _____ is a mathematical technique that uses historical results to predict future outcome.

   a. Trend analysis
   b. Multicollinearity
   c. 3M Company
   d. Regression analysis

13. _____ is the process of comparing the cost, cycle time, productivity, or quality of a specific process or method to another that is widely considered to be an industry standard or best practice. Essentially, _____ provides a snapshot of the performance of your business and helps you understand where you are in relation to a particular standard. The result is often a business case for making changes in order to make improvements.
   a. Benchmarking
   b. Strategic business unit
   c. 3M Company
   d. BMC Software, Inc.

14. _____ is a process used to manage information technology (IT). Its primary goal is to ensure that IT capacity meets current and future business requirements in a cost-effective manner. One common interpretation of _____ is described in the ITIL framework. ITIL version 3 views _____ as comprising three sub-processes: business _____, service _____, and component _____.
   a. 3M Company
   b. BMC Software, Inc.
   c. BNSF Railway
   d. Capacity management

15. In probability theory and statistics, the _____ of a random variable, probability distribution averaging the squared distance of its possible values from the expected value (mean.) Whereas the mean is a way to describe the location of a distribution, the _____ is a way to capture its scale or degree of being spread out. The unit of _____ is the square of the unit of the original variable.
   a. Monte Carlo methods
   b. Time series
   c. Statistics
   d. Variance

16. An _____ is a practitioner of accountancy, which is the measurement, disclosure or provision of assurance about financial information that helps managers, investors, tax authorities and other decision makers make resource allocation decisions.

The word '_____' is derived from the French 'Compter' which took its origin from the Latin 'Computare'. The word was formerly written in English as 'Accomptant', but in process of time the word, which was always pronounced by dropping the 'p', became gradually changed both in pronunciation and in orthography to its present form.

Chapter 5. Activity-Based Management

a. AMEX
b. Accountant
c. AIG
d. ABC Television Network

17. The _____ is a professional organization headquartered in Montvale, New Jersey consisting of over 70,000 members worldwide. The IMA is dedicated to advancing the role of the management accountant and financial manager within the business organization, and provides relevant professional certification.

The IMA awards the Certified Management Accountant (CMA) designation in the United States.

a. International Accounting Standards Committee
b. Emerging technologies
c. American Accounting Association
d. Institute of Management Accountants

18. _____ is concerned with the provisions and use of accounting information to managers within organizations, to provide them with the basis to make informed business decisions that will allow them to be better equipped in their management and control functions.

In contrast to financial accountancy information, _____ information is:

- usually confidential and used by management, instead of publicly reported;
- forward-looking, instead of historical;
- pragmatically computed using extensive management information systems and internal controls, instead of complying with accounting standards.

This is because of the different emphasis: _____ information is used within an organization, typically for decision-making.

a. Governmental accounting
b. Nonassurance services
c. Grenzplankostenrechnung
d. Management accounting

19. A _____, also client, buyer or purchaser is the buyer or user of the paid products of an individual or organization, mostly called the supplier or seller. This is typically through purchasing or renting goods or services.

a. BMC Software, Inc.
b. BNSF Railway
c. Customer
d. 3M Company

Chapter 6. Job-Order and Process Costing

1. _____ is an accounting methodology that traces and accumulates direct costs, and allocates indirect costs of a manufacturing process. Costs are assigned to products, usually in a large batch, which might include an entire month's production. Eventually, costs have to be allocated to individual units of product.
   a. Process costing
   b. Profit center
   c. Cost driver
   d. Cost management

2. _____ refers to a business or organization attempting to acquire goods or services to accomplish the goals of the enterprise. Though there are several organizations that attempt to set standards in the _____ process, processes can vary greatly between organizations. Typically the word e;_____e; is not used interchangeably with the word e;procuremente;, since procurement typically includes Expediting, Supplier Quality, and Traffic and Logistics (T'L) in addition to _____.
   a. Consignor
   b. Free port
   c. Supply chain
   d. Purchasing

3. The _____ is a performance management tool which began as a concept for measuring whether the smaller-scale operational activities of a company are aligned with its larger-scale objectives in terms of vision and strategy.

   By focusing not only on financial outcomes but also on the operational, marketing and developmental inputs to these, the _____ helps provide a more comprehensive view of a business, which in turn helps organizations act in their best long-term interests. This tool is also being used to address business response to climate change and greenhouse gas emissions.

   a. Best practice
   b. Management by objectives
   c. Trustee
   d. Balanced Scorecard

4. In economics, business, retail, and accounting, a _____ is the value of money that has been used up to produce something, and hence is not available for use anymore. In economics, a _____ is an alternative that is given up as a result of a decision. In business, the _____ may be one of acquisition, in which case the amount of money expended to acquire it is counted as _____.
   a. Cost of quality
   b. Cost allocation
   c. Prime cost
   d. Cost

5. In financial accounting, a _____ is defined as an obligation of an entity arising from past transactions or events, the settlement of which may result in the transfer or use of assets, provision of services or other yielding of economic benefits in the future.
   a. Vested
   b. Corporate governance
   c. Liability
   d. False Claims Act

6. _____ is concerned with the provisions and use of accounting information to managers within organizations, to provide them with the basis to make informed business decisions that will allow them to be better equipped in their management and control functions.

In contrast to financial accountancy information, _____ information is:

- usually confidential and used by management, instead of publicly reported;
- forward-looking, instead of historical;
- pragmatically computed using extensive management information systems and internal controls, instead of complying with accounting standards.

This is because of the different emphasis: _____ information is used within an organization, typically for decision-making.

a. Grenzplankostenrechnung
c. Nonassurance services
b. Management Accounting
d. Governmental accounting

7. The _____ is a private, not-for-profit organization whose primary purpose is to develop generally accepted accounting principles (GAAP) within the United States in the public's interest. The Securities and Exchange Commission (SEC) designated the _____ as the organization responsible for setting accounting standards for public companies in the U.S. It was created in 1973, replacing the Accounting Principles Board and the Committee on Accounting Procedure of the American Institute of Certified Public Accountants. The _____'s mission is 'to establish and improve standards of financial accounting and reporting for the guidance and education of the public, including issuers, auditors, and users of financial information.'

The _____ is not a governmental body.

a. Governmental Accounting Standards Board
c. Fannie Mae
b. Financial Accounting Standards Board
d. Public company

8. _____s are goods that have completed the manufacturing process but have not yet been sold or distributed to the end user.

Manufacturing has three classes of inventory:

1. Raw material
2. Work in process
3. _____s

A good purchased as a 'raw material' goes into the manufacture of a product. A good only partially completed during the manufacturing process is called 'work in process'. When the good is completed as to manufacturing but not yet sold or distributed to the end-user is called a '_____'.

a. Finished good
c. Reorder point
b. FIFO and LIFO accounting
d. 3M Company

Chapter 6. Job-Order and Process Costing

9. In financial accounting, _____ or cost of sales includes the direct costs attributable to the production of the goods sold by a company. This amount includes the materials cost used in creating the goods along with the direct labor costs used to produce the good. It excludes indirect expenses such as distribution costs and sales force costs.
   a. FIFO and LIFO accounting
   b. 3M Company
   c. Cost of goods sold
   d. Reorder point

10. A _____ is an entity formed between two or more parties to undertake economic activity together. The parties agree to create a new entity by both contributing equity, and they then share in the revenues, expenses, and control of the enterprise. The venture can be for one specific project only, or a continuing business relationship such as the Fuji Xerox _____.
    a. Joint venture
    b. Fraud Enforcement and Recovery Act
    c. Pre-emption right
    d. Chief Financial Officers Act of 1990

11. A _____ is a fungible, negotiable instrument representing financial value. they are broadly categorized into debt securities (such as banknotes, bonds and debentures), and equity securities; e.g., common stocks. The company or other entity issuing the _____ is called the issuer.
    a. 3M Company
    b. Tracking stock
    c. BMC Software, Inc.
    d. Security

12. The U.S. _____ is an independent agency of the United States government which holds primary responsibility for enforcing the federal securities laws and regulating the securities industry, the nation's stock and options exchanges, and other electronic securities markets. The SEC was created by section 4 of the Securities Exchange Act of 1934 (now codified as 15 U.S.C. ÂÂ§ 78d and commonly referred to as the 1934 Act.)
    a. 3M Company
    b. BNSF Railway
    c. BMC Software, Inc.
    d. Securities and Exchange Commission

13. _____ is an acronym for First In, First Out, an abstraction in ways of organizing and manipulation of data relative to time and prioritization. This expression describes the principle of a queue processing technique or servicing conflicting demands by ordering process by first-come, first-served (FCFS) behaviour: what comes in first is handled first, what comes in next waits until the first is finished, etc.

    Thus it is analogous to the behaviour of persons queueing (or 'standing in line', in common American parlance), where the persons leave the queue in the order they arrive, or waiting one's turn at a traffic control signal.

    a. Risk management
    b. Trademark
    c. Kanban
    d. FIFO

14. Under the _____, it is assumed that the cost of inventory is based on the average cost of the goods available for sale during the period. Average cost is computed by dividing the total cost of goods available for sale by the total units available for sale. This gives a weighted-average unit cost that is applied to the units in the ending inventory.
    a. Average-cost method
    b. AMEX
    c. ABC Television Network
    d. AIG

15. An _____ is a term used in behavioral economics to describe those types of behaviors that impose costs on a person in the long-run that are not taken into account when making decisions in the present. Classical Economics discourages government from creating legislation that targets internalities, because it is assumed that the consumer takes these personal costs into account when paying for the good that causes the _____. For example, cigarettes should be taxed because of the negative consumption externalities that they impose, such as second-hand smoke, not because the smoker harms him or herself by smoking.

a. Internality
b. Inventory turnover ratio
c. Operating budget
d. Authorised capital

16. The _____ is the United States federal government agency that collects taxes and enforces the internal revenue laws. It is an agency within the U.S. Dept of the treasury responsible for interpretation and application of Federal tax law. The official U.S. Treasury regulations provide (in part):

The _____ is a bureau of the Department of the Treasury under the immediate direction of the Commissioner of Internal Revenue.

a. Income tax
b. Indirect tax
c. Use tax
d. Internal Revenue Service

17. In finance, _____ is the process of estimating the potential market value of a financial asset or liability. They can be done on assets (for example, investments in marketable securities such as stocks, options, business enterprises, or intangible assets such as patents and trademarks) or on liabilities (e.g., Bonds issued by a company.) A _____ is required in many contexts including investment analysis, capital budgeting, merger and acquisition transactions, financial reporting, taxable events to determine the proper tax liability, and in litigation.

a. Vyborg Appeal
b. Daybook
c. Valuation
d. Disclosure

18. _____ is systematic determination of merit, worth, and significance of something or someone using criteria against a set of standards. _____ often is used to characterize and appraise subjects of interest in a wide range of human enterprises, including the arts, criminal justice, foundations and non-profit organizations, government, health care, and other human services.

Depending on the topic of interest, there are professional groups which look to the quality and rigor of the _____ process.

a. ABC Television Network
b. AIG
c. Evaluation
d. AMEX

19. An _____ is a classification used for business units within an enterprise. The essential element of an _____ is that it is treated as a unit which is measured against its use of capital, as opposed to a cost or profit center, which are measured against raw costs or profits.

The advantage of this form of measurement is that it tends to be more encompassing, since it accounts for all uses of capital.

a. AMEX
b. AIG
c. ABC Television Network
d. Investment center

20. A _____ has several related meanings:

- a daily record of events or business; a private _____ is usually referred to as a diary.
- a newspaper or other periodical, in the literal sense of one published each day;
- many publications issued at stated intervals, such as magazines, or scholarly academic _____s, or the record of the transactions of a society, are often called _____s. Although _____ is sometimes used, erroneously, as a synonym for 'magazine,' in academic use, a _____ refers to a serious, scholarly publication, most often peer-reviewed. A non-scholarly magazine written for an educated audience about an industry or an area of professional activity is usually called a professional magazine.

The word 'journalist' for one whose business is writing for the public press has been in use since the end of the 17th century.

Open access _____s are scholarly _____s that are available to the reader without financial or other barrier other than access to the internet itself. Some are subsidized, and some require payment on behalf of the author. Subsidized _____s are financed by an academic institution or a government information center.

a. BNSF Railway
b. Journal
c. BMC Software, Inc.
d. 3M Company

Chapter 7. Support-Department Cost Allocation

1. An _____ is a practitioner of accountancy, which is the measurement, disclosure or provision of assurance about financial information that helps managers, investors, tax authorities and other decision makers make resource allocation decisions.

The word '_____' is derived from the French 'Compter' which took its origin from the Latin 'Computare'. The word was formerly written in English as 'Accomptant', but in process of time the word, which was always pronounced by dropping the 'p', became gradually changed both in pronunciation and in orthography to its present form.

 a. Accountant
 b. ABC Television Network
 c. AMEX
 d. AIG

2. The _____ is a professional organization headquartered in Montvale, New Jersey consisting of over 70,000 members worldwide. The IMA is dedicated to advancing the role of the management accountant and financial manager within the business organization, and provides relevant professional certification.

The IMA awards the Certified Management Accountant (CMA) designation in the United States.

 a. International Accounting Standards Committee
 b. American Accounting Association
 c. Emerging technologies
 d. Institute of Management Accountants

3. _____ is concerned with the provisions and use of accounting information to managers within organizations, to provide them with the basis to make informed business decisions that will allow them to be better equipped in their management and control functions.

In contrast to financial accountancy information, _____ information is:

- usually confidential and used by management, instead of publicly reported;
- forward-looking, instead of historical;
- pragmatically computed using extensive management information systems and internal controls, instead of complying with accounting standards.

This is because of the different emphasis: _____ information is used within an organization, typically for decision-making.

 a. Nonassurance services
 b. Grenzplankostenrechnung
 c. Governmental accounting
 d. Management accounting

4. In economics, business, retail, and accounting, a _____ is the value of money that has been used up to produce something, and hence is not available for use anymore. In economics, a _____ is an alternative that is given up as a result of a decision. In business, the _____ may be one of acquisition, in which case the amount of money expended to acquire it is counted as _____.

 a. Prime cost
 b. Cost of quality
 c. Cost
 d. Cost allocation

Chapter 7. Support-Department Cost Allocation

5. _____ is a process of attributing cost to particular cost centres. For example the wage of the driver of the purchasing department can be allocated to the purchasing department cost centre. It is not necessary to share the wage cost over several different cost centers.

   a. Variable cost
   b. Cost of quality
   c. Cost allocation
   d. Cost accounting

6. The _____ is a performance management tool which began as a concept for measuring whether the smaller-scale operational activities of a company are aligned with its larger-scale objectives in terms of vision and strategy.

   By focusing not only on financial outcomes but also on the operational, marketing and developmental inputs to these, the _____ helps provide a more comprehensive view of a business, which in turn helps organizations act in their best long-term interests. This tool is also being used to address business response to climate change and greenhouse gas emissions.

   a. Management by objectives
   b. Trustee
   c. Balanced Scorecard
   d. Best practice

7. _____ is the acquisition of goods and/or services at the best possible total cost of ownership, in the right quantity and quality, at the right time, in the right place and from the right source for the direct benefit or use of corporations or individuals, generally via a contract. Simple _____ may involve nothing more than repeat purchasing. Complex _____ could involve finding long term partners - or even 'co-destiny' suppliers that might fundamentally commit one organization to another.

   a. Free cash flow
   b. Procurement
   c. Time to market
   d. Customer satisfaction

8. _____ is an acronym for First In, First Out, an abstraction in ways of organizing and manipulation of data relative to time and prioritization. This expression describes the principle of a queue processing technique or servicing conflicting demands by ordering process by first-come, first-served (FCFS) behaviour: what comes in first is handled first, what comes in next waits until the first is finished, etc.

   Thus it is analogous to the behaviour of persons queueing (or 'standing in line', in common American parlance), where the persons leave the queue in the order they arrive, or waiting one's turn at a traffic control signal.

   a. Kanban
   b. FIFO
   c. Trademark
   d. Risk management

9. A _____ is a fungible, negotiable instrument representing financial value. they are broadly categorized into debt securities (such as banknotes, bonds and debentures), and equity securities; e.g., common stocks. The company or other entity issuing the _____ is called the issuer.

   a. 3M Company
   b. BMC Software, Inc.
   c. Tracking stock
   d. Security

10. The U.S. _____ is an independent agency of the United States government which holds primary responsibility for enforcing the federal securities laws and regulating the securities industry, the nation's stock and options exchanges, and other electronic securities markets. The SEC was created by section 4 of the Securities Exchange Act of 1934 (now codified as 15 U.S.C. ÂÂ§ 78d and commonly referred to as the 1934 Act.)

Chapter 7. Support-Department Cost Allocation

a. BNSF Railway
b. BMC Software, Inc.
c. 3M Company
d. Securities and Exchange Commission

11. In mathematics _____s are numbers or other things that get multiplied. In particular, see:

- Factorization, the decomposition of an object into a product of other objects
- Integer factorization, the process of breaking down a composite number into smaller non-trivial divisors
- A coefficient
- A divisor of a particular number, or of an element of a monoid
- A von Neumann algebra with a trivial center

In statistics

- _____ analysis is the study of how _____s or certain variables affect variables.

In technology:

- Human _____s, a profession that focuses on how people interact with products, tools, or procedures
- 'Functionality, Application domain, Conditions, Technology, Objects and Responsibility;', In object-oriented programming

In computer science and information technology:

- Authentication _____, a piece of information used to verify a person's identity for security purposes
- _____, a Unix command for numbers factorization
- _____ (programming language), an experimental Forth-like programming language

In television:

- The O'Reilly _____, an American talk show hosted by Bill O'Reilly on Fox News.
- The Krypton _____, a British game show hosted by Gordon Burns, formally on ITV. Also had an American version.

a. Merck ' Co., Inc.
b. Valuation
c. The Goodyear Tire ' Rubber Company
d. Factor

12. A _____ is an entity formed between two or more parties to undertake economic activity together. The parties agree to create a new entity by both contributing equity, and they then share in the revenues, expenses, and control of the enterprise. The venture can be for one specific project only, or a continuing business relationship such as the Fuji Xerox _____.

a. Pre-emption right
b. Fraud Enforcement and Recovery Act
c. Chief Financial Officers Act of 1990
d. Joint venture

Chapter 7. Support-Department Cost Allocation

13. In business, _____, Overhead cost or _____ expense refers to an ongoing expense of operating a business. The term _____ is usually used to group expenses that are necessary to the continued functioning of the business, but do not directly generate profits.

_____ expenses are all costs on the income statement except for direct labor and direct materials.

a. ABC Television Network
c. Overhead
b. Intangible assets
d. AIG

14. _____ refers to a business or organization attempting to acquire goods or services to accomplish the goals of the enterprise. Though there are several organizations that attempt to set standards in the _____ process, processes can vary greatly between organizations. Typically the word e;_____e; is not used interchangeably with the word e;procuremente;, since procurement typically includes Expediting, Supplier Quality, and Traffic and Logistics (T'L) in addition to _____.

a. Consignor
c. Supply chain
b. Free port
d. Purchasing

15. In economics ' business, specifically cost accounting, the _____ is the point at which cost or expenses and revenue are equal: there is no net loss or gain, and one has 'broken even'. A profit or a loss has not been made, although opportunity costs have been paid, and capital has received the risk-adjusted, expected return.

For example, if the business sells less than 200 tables each month, it will make a loss, if it sells more, it will be a profit.

a. Break-even point
c. BMC Software, Inc.
b. Defined benefit pension plan
d. 3M Company

16. A _____ is the pinnacle activity involved in selling products or services in return for money or other compensation. It is an act of completion of a commercial activity.

A _____ is completed by the seller, the owner of the goods.

a. High yield stock
c. Maturity
b. Sale
d. Tertiary sector of economy

17. A _____ is a secondary or incidental product deriving from a manufacturing process, a chemical reaction or a biochemical pathway, and is not the primary product or service being produced. A _____ can be useful and marketable, or it can have negative ecological impact.

- dried blood and blood meal - from slaughterhouse operations
- chicken _____ meal - clean parts of the carcass of slaughtered chicken, such as necks, feet, undeveloped eggs, and intestines.
- chrome shavings - from a stage of leather manufacture
- collagen and gelatin - from the boiled skin and other parts of slaughtered livestock
- feathers - from poultry processing
    - feather meal - from poultry processing
- lanolin - from the cleaning of wool
- manure - from animal husbandry
- meat and bone meal - from the rendering of animal bones and offal
- poultry byproduct and poultry meal - made from unmarketable poultry bones and offal
- poultry litter - swept from the floors of chicken coops
- whey - from cheese manufacturing
- fetal pigs

- acidulated soap stock - from the refining of vegetable oil
- bran and germ - from the milling of whole grains into refined grains
- brewer's yeast - from ethanol fermentation
- cereal food fines - from breakfast cereal processing
- corn stover - residual plant matter after harvesting of cereals
- distillers grains - from ethanol fermentation
- glycerol - from the production of biodiesel
- grape seed oil - recovered from leftovers of the winemaking process
- molasses - from sugar refining
- orange oil and other citrus oils - recovered from the peels of processed fruit
- pectin - recovered from the remains of processed fruit
- sawdust and bark- from the processing of logs into lumber
- soybean meal - from soybean processing
- straw- from grain harvesting

- asphalt - from the refining of crude oil
- fly ash - from the combustion of coal
- slag - from ore refining
- gypsum - from Flue gas desulfurization
- ash and smoke - from the combustion of fuel
- mineral oil - from refining crude oil to produce gasoline
- salt - from desalination

- sludge - from wastewater treatment

a. BMC Software, Inc.
b. By-product
c. 3M Company
d. BNSF Railway

18. _____ is a method of evaluating an asset's worth when held in inventory, in the field of accounting. _____ is part of the Generally Accepted Accounting Principles that apply to valuing inventory, so as to not overstate or understate the value of inventory goods. Net realisable value is generally equal to the selling price of the inventory goods less the selling costs (completion and disposal).

a. BMC Software, Inc.
b. 3M Company
c. Revenue recognition
d. Net realizable value

Chapter 8. Budgeting for Planning and Control

1. An _____ is a practitioner of accountancy, which is the measurement, disclosure or provision of assurance about financial information that helps managers, investors, tax authorities and other decision makers make resource allocation decisions.

The word '_____' is derived from the French 'Compter' which took its origin from the Latin 'Computare'. The word was formerly written in English as 'Accomptant', but in process of time the word, which was always pronounced by dropping the 'p', became gradually changed both in pronunciation and in orthography to its present form.

   a. ABC Television Network
   b. AMEX
   c. Accountant
   d. AIG

2. The _____ is a professional organization headquartered in Montvale, New Jersey consisting of over 70,000 members worldwide. The IMA is dedicated to advancing the role of the management accountant and financial manager within the business organization, and provides relevant professional certification.

The IMA awards the Certified Management Accountant (CMA) designation in the United States.

   a. Emerging technologies
   b. International Accounting Standards Committee
   c. American Accounting Association
   d. Institute of Management Accountants

3. _____ is concerned with the provisions and use of accounting information to managers within organizations, to provide them with the basis to make informed business decisions that will allow them to be better equipped in their management and control functions.

In contrast to financial accountancy information, _____ information is:

   - usually confidential and used by management, instead of publicly reported;
   - forward-looking, instead of historical;
   - pragmatically computed using extensive management information systems and internal controls, instead of complying with accounting standards.

This is because of the different emphasis: _____ information is used within an organization, typically for decision-making.

   a. Nonassurance services
   b. Management accounting
   c. Governmental accounting
   d. Grenzplankostenrechnung

4. Project _____: The project _____ is a prediction of the costs associated with a particular company project. These costs include labor, materials, and other related expenses. The project _____ is often broken down into specific tasks, with task _____s assigned to each.
   a. BMC Software, Inc.
   b. 3M Company
   c. BNSF Railway
   d. Budget

5. In financial accounting, a _____ is defined as an obligation of an entity arising from past transactions or events, the settlement of which may result in the transfer or use of assets, provision of services or other yielding of economic benefits in the future.

Chapter 8. Budgeting for Planning and Control 41

a. False Claims Act
b. Liability
c. Vested
d. Corporate governance

6. The _____ is a private, not-for-profit organization whose primary purpose is to develop generally accepted accounting principles (GAAP) within the United States in the public's interest. The Securities and Exchange Commission (SEC) designated the _____ as the organization responsible for setting accounting standards for public companies in the U.S. It was created in 1973, replacing the Accounting Principles Board and the Committee on Accounting Procedure of the American Institute of Certified Public Accountants. The _____'s mission is 'to establish and improve standards of financial accounting and reporting for the guidance and education of the public, including issuers, auditors, and users of financial information.'

The _____ is not a governmental body.

a. Governmental Accounting Standards Board
b. Public company
c. Fannie Mae
d. Financial Accounting Standards Board

7. An _____ is the annual budget of an activity stated in terms of Budget Classification Code, functional/subfunctional categories and cost accounts. It contains estimates of the total value of resources required for the performance of the operation including reimbursable work or services for others. It also includes estimates of workload in terms of total work units identified by cost accounts.

a. Inventory turnover ratio
b. Internality
c. Operating budget
d. Authorised capital

8. A _____ is the pinnacle activity involved in selling products or services in return for money or other compensation. It is an act of completion of a commercial activity.

A _____ is completed by the seller, the owner of the goods.

a. Tertiary sector of economy
b. Maturity
c. High yield stock
d. Sale

9. The _____ is a performance management tool which began as a concept for measuring whether the smaller-scale operational activities of a company are aligned with its larger-scale objectives in terms of vision and strategy.

By focusing not only on financial outcomes but also on the operational, marketing and developmental inputs to these, the _____ helps provide a more comprehensive view of a business, which in turn helps organizations act in their best long-term interests. This tool is also being used to address business response to climate change and greenhouse gas emissions.

a. Best practice
b. Management by objectives
c. Trustee
d. Balanced Scorecard

10. A film _____ determines how much money will be spent on the entire film project. It involves the identification and estimation of cost items for each phase of filmmaking (development, pre-production, production, post-production and distribution.)

The budget structure is normally split into 'above-the-line' (creative) and 'below-the-line' (technical) costs.

a. BNSF Railway
b. BMC Software, Inc.
c. 3M Company
d. Production budget

11. _____ refers to a business or organization attempting to acquire goods or services to accomplish the goals of the enterprise. Though there are several organizations that attempt to set standards in the _____ process, processes can vary greatly between organizations. Typically the word e;_____e; is not used interchangeably with the word e;procuremente;, since procurement typically includes Expediting, Supplier Quality, and Traffic and Logistics (T'L) in addition to _____.

a. Purchasing
b. Supply chain
c. Free port
d. Consignor

12. _____ is a costing model that identifies activities in an organization and assigns the cost of each activity resource to all products and services according to the actual consumption by each: it assigns more indirect costs (overhead) into direct costs.

In this way an organization can establish the true cost of its individual products and services for the purposes of identifying and eliminating those which are unprofitable and lowering the prices of those which are overpriced.

In a business organization, the ABC methodology assigns an organization's resource costs through activities to the products and services provided to its customers.

a. ABC Television Network
b. Indirect costs
c. Activity-based management
d. Activity-based costing

13. _____s are goods that have completed the manufacturing process but have not yet been sold or distributed to the end user.

Manufacturing has three classes of inventory:

1. Raw material
2. Work in process
3. _____s

A good purchased as a 'raw material' goes into the manufacture of a product. A good only partially completed during the manufacturing process is called 'work in process'. When the good is completed as to manufacturing but not yet sold or distributed to the end-user is called a '_____'.

a. Finished good
b. FIFO and LIFO accounting
c. 3M Company
d. Reorder point

Chapter 8. Budgeting for Planning and Control

14. In business, _____, Overhead cost or _____ expense refers to an ongoing expense of operating a business. The term _____ is usually used to group expenses that are necessary to the continued functioning of the business, but do not directly generate profits.

_____ expenses are all costs on the income statement except for direct labor and direct materials.

a. ABC Television Network
c. Intangible assets
b. AIG
d. Overhead

15. A _____ is a fungible, negotiable instrument representing financial value. they are broadly categorized into debt securities (such as banknotes, bonds and debentures), and equity securities; e.g., common stocks. The company or other entity issuing the _____ is called the issuer.

a. Tracking stock
c. BMC Software, Inc.
b. 3M Company
d. Security

16. The U.S. _____ is an independent agency of the United States government which holds primary responsibility for enforcing the federal securities laws and regulating the securities industry, the nation's stock and options exchanges, and other electronic securities markets. The SEC was created by section 4 of the Securities Exchange Act of 1934 (now codified as 15 U.S.C. ÂÂ§ 78d and commonly referred to as the 1934 Act.)

a. Securities and Exchange Commission
c. BNSF Railway
b. BMC Software, Inc.
d. 3M Company

17. In economics, business, retail, and accounting, a _____ is the value of money that has been used up to produce something, and hence is not available for use anymore. In economics, a _____ is an alternative that is given up as a result of a decision. In business, the _____ may be one of acquisition, in which case the amount of money expended to acquire it is counted as _____.

a. Prime cost
c. Cost
b. Cost allocation
d. Cost of quality

18. In financial accounting, _____ or cost of sales includes the direct costs attributable to the production of the goods sold by a company. This amount includes the materials cost used in creating the goods along with the direct labor costs used to produce the good. It excludes indirect expenses such as distribution costs and sales force costs.

a. Cost of goods sold
c. FIFO and LIFO accounting
b. 3M Company
d. Reorder point

19. In accounting, _____ has a very specific meaning. It is an outflow of cash or other valuable assets from a person or company to another person or company. This outflow of cash is generally one side of a trade for products or services that have equal or better current or future value to the buyer than to the seller.

a. AIG
c. AMEX
b. ABC Television Network
d. Expense

20. In economics, _____ or _____ goods or real _____ refers to factors of production used to create goods or services that are not themselves significantly consumed (though they may depreciate) in the production process. _____ goods may be acquired with money or financial _____. In finance and accounting, _____ generally refers to financial wealth, especially that used to start or maintain a business.

a. Screening
b. Capital
c. Disclosure
d. Vyborg Appeal

21. _____ is the planning process used to determine whether a firm's long term investments such as new machinery, replacement machinery, new plants, new products, and research development projects are worth pursuing. It is budget for major capital, or investment, expenditures.

Many formal methods are used in _____, including the techniques such as

- Net present value
- Profitability index
- Internal rate of return
- Modified Internal Rate of Return
- Equivalent annuity

These methods use the incremental cash flows from each potential investment, or project. Techniques based on accounting earnings and accounting rules are sometimes used - though economists consider this to be improper - such as the accounting rate of return, and 'return on investment.' Simplified and hybrid methods are used as well, such as payback period and discounted payback period.

a. Capital budgeting
b. Preferred stock
c. Cash flow
d. Gross profit

22. _____ is a company's financial statement that indicates how the revenue is transformed into the net income The purpose of the _____ is to show managers and investors whether the company made or lost money during the period being reported.

The important thing to remember about an _____ is that it represents a period of time.

a. ABC Television Network
b. AIG
c. Income statement
d. AMEX

23. _____ is a term used in accounting, economics and finance to spread the cost of an asset over the span of several years.

In simple words we can say that _____ is the reduction in the value of an asset due to usage, passage of time, wear and tear, technological outdating or obsolescence, depletion, inadequacy, rot, rust, decay or other such factors.

In accounting, _____ is a term used to describe any method of attributing the historical or purchase cost of an asset across its useful life, roughly corresponding to normal wear and tear.

a. Depreciation
b. Current asset
c. General ledger
d. Net profit

Chapter 8. Budgeting for Planning and Control

24. In financial accounting, a _____ or statement of financial position is a summary of a person's or organization's balances. Assets, liabilities and ownership equity are listed as of a specific date, such as the end of its financial year. A _____ is often described as a snapshot of a company's financial condition.
   a. 3M Company
   b. Balance sheet
   c. Financial statements
   d. Statement of retained earnings

25. _____ is systematic determination of merit, worth, and significance of something or someone using criteria against a set of standards. _____ often is used to characterize and appraise subjects of interest in a wide range of human enterprises, including the arts, criminal justice, foundations and non-profit organizations, government, health care, and other human services.

Depending on the topic of interest, there are professional groups which look to the quality and rigor of the _____ process.

   a. AIG
   b. ABC Television Network
   c. AMEX
   d. Evaluation

26. _____ is an acronym for First In, First Out, an abstraction in ways of organizing and manipulation of data relative to time and prioritization. This expression describes the principle of a queue processing technique or servicing conflicting demands by ordering process by first-come, first-served (FCFS) behaviour: what comes in first is handled first, what comes in next waits until the first is finished, etc.

Thus it is analogous to the behaviour of persons queueing (or 'standing in line', in common American parlance), where the persons leave the queue in the order they arrive, or waiting one's turn at a traffic control signal.

   a. Trademark
   b. Risk management
   c. FIFO
   d. Kanban

27. In economics, _____ are business expenses that are not dependent on the activities of the business They tend to be time-related, such as salaries or rents being paid per month. This is in contrast to variable costs, which are volume-related (and are paid per quantity.)

In management accounting, _____ are defined as expenses that do not change in proportion to the activity of a business, within the relevant period or scale of production.

   a. Fixed costs
   b. Cost accounting
   c. Marginal cost
   d. Cost of quality

28. _____s are expenses that change in proportion to the activity of a business. In other words, _____ is the sum of marginal costs. It can also be considered normal costs.
   a. Variable cost
   b. Quality costs
   c. Cost accounting
   d. Fixed costs

29. _____ is the term used to refer to the standard framework of guidelines for financial accounting used in any given jurisdiction. _____ includes the standards, conventions, and rules accountants follow in recording and summarizing transactions, and in the preparation of financial statements.

Financial accounting information must be assembled and reported objectively.

    a. Generally Accepted Accounting Principles
    b. Current asset
    c. Long-term liabilities
    d. General ledger

30. In economics and sociology, an _____ is any factor (financial or non-financial) that enables or motivates a particular course of action, or counts as a reason for preferring one choice to the alternatives. It is an expectation that encourages people to behave in a certain way. Since human beings are purposeful creatures, the study of _____ structures is central to the study of all economic activity (both in terms of individual decision-making and in terms of co-operation and competition within a larger institutional structure.)
    a. ABC Television Network
    b. AIG
    c. AMEX
    d. Incentive

31. A _____ is an entity formed between two or more parties to undertake economic activity together. The parties agree to create a new entity by both contributing equity, and they then share in the revenues, expenses, and control of the enterprise. The venture can be for one specific project only, or a continuing business relationship such as the Fuji Xerox _____.
    a. Chief Financial Officers Act of 1990
    b. Joint venture
    c. Fraud Enforcement and Recovery Act
    d. Pre-emption right

Chapter 9. Standard Costing: A Managerial Control Tool

1. The _____ is a performance management tool which began as a concept for measuring whether the smaller-scale operational activities of a company are aligned with its larger-scale objectives in terms of vision and strategy.

By focusing not only on financial outcomes but also on the operational, marketing and developmental inputs to these, the _____ helps provide a more comprehensive view of a business, which in turn helps organizations act in their best long-term interests. This tool is also being used to address business response to climate change and greenhouse gas emissions.

a. Best practice
b. Management by objectives
c. Trustee
d. Balanced Scorecard

2. _____ is an acronym for First In, First Out, an abstraction in ways of organizing and manipulation of data relative to time and prioritization. This expression describes the principle of a queue processing technique or servicing conflicting demands by ordering process by first-come, first-served (FCFS) behaviour: what comes in first is handled first, what comes in next waits until the first is finished, etc.

Thus it is analogous to the behaviour of persons queueing (or 'standing in line', in common American parlance), where the persons leave the queue in the order they arrive, or waiting one's turn at a traffic control signal.

a. Risk management
b. Kanban
c. FIFO
d. Trademark

3. _____ in economics and business is the result of an exchange and from that trade we assign a numerical monetary value to a good, service or asset. If Alice trades Bob 4 apples for an orange, the _____ of an orange is 4 apples. Inversely, the _____ of an apple is 1/4 oranges.

a. Price discrimination
b. Discounts and allowances
c. Transactional Net Margin Method
d. Price

4. In economics, business, retail, and accounting, a _____ is the value of money that has been used up to produce something, and hence is not available for use anymore. In economics, a _____ is an alternative that is given up as a result of a decision. In business, the _____ may be one of acquisition, in which case the amount of money expended to acquire it is counted as _____.

a. Cost
b. Cost of quality
c. Cost allocation
d. Prime cost

5. Project _____: The project _____ is a prediction of the costs associated with a particular company project. These costs include labor, materials, and other related expenses. The project _____ is often broken down into specific tasks, with task _____s assigned to each.

a. BMC Software, Inc.
b. 3M Company
c. BNSF Railway
d. Budget

6. The materials _____ is computed as follows:

Vmp = (Actual Unit Cost - Standard Unit Cost) * Actual Quantity Purchased or

$$V_{mp} = (\text{Actual Quantity Purchased} * \text{Actual Unit Cost}) - (\text{Actual Quantity Purchased} * \text{Standard Unit Cost.})$$

When the Actual Materials Price is higher than the Standard Materials Price, the variance is said to be unfavorable, since the Actual price paid on materials purchased is greater than the allowed standard. The variance is said to be favorable when the Standard materials Price is higher than the Actual Materials Price, since less money was spent in purchasing the materials than the allowed standard.

a. Price variance
b. Fund accounting
c. Liquidating dividend
d. Consolidated financial statements

7. In probability theory and statistics, the _____ of a random variable, probability distribution averaging the squared distance of its possible values from the expected value (mean.) Whereas the mean is a way to describe the location of a distribution, the _____ is a way to capture its scale or degree of being spread out. The unit of _____ is the square of the unit of the original variable.

a. Statistics
b. Monte Carlo methods
c. Time series
d. Variance

8. In statistics, _____ (ANOVA) is a collection of statistical models, and their associated procedures, in which the observed variance is partitioned into components due to different explanatory variables. In its simplest form ANOVA gives a statistical test of whether the means of several groups are all equal, and therefore generalizes Student's two-sample t-test to more than two groups.

There are three conceptual classes of such models:

1. Fixed-effects models assumes that the data came from normal populations which may differ only in their means. (Model 1)
2. Random effects models assume that the data describe a hierarchy of different populations whose differences are constrained by the hierarchy. (Model 2)
3. Mixed-effect models describe situations where both fixed and random effects are present. (Model 3)

In practice, there are several types of ANOVA depending on the number of treatments and the way they are applied to the subjects in the experiment:

- One-way ANOVA is used to test for differences among two or more independent groups. Typically, however, the one-way ANOVA is used to test for differences among at least three groups, since the two-group case can be covered by a T-test (Gossett, 1908.)

a. Intergenerational equity
b. IMF
c. Open database connectivity
d. Analysis of variance

Chapter 9. Standard Costing: A Managerial Control Tool 49

9. In financial accounting, a _____ is defined as an obligation of an entity arising from past transactions or events, the settlement of which may result in the transfer or use of assets, provision of services or other yielding of economic benefits in the future.

    a. Corporate governance   b. Vested
    c. False Claims Act   d. Liability

10. The _____ is a private, not-for-profit organization whose primary purpose is to develop generally accepted accounting principles (GAAP) within the United States in the public's interest. The Securities and Exchange Commission (SEC) designated the _____ as the organization responsible for setting accounting standards for public companies in the U.S. It was created in 1973, replacing the Accounting Principles Board and the Committee on Accounting Procedure of the American Institute of Certified Public Accountants. The _____'s mission is 'to establish and improve standards of financial accounting and reporting for the guidance and education of the public, including issuers, auditors, and users of financial information.'

The _____ is not a governmental body.

    a. Public company   b. Financial Accounting Standards Board
    c. Fannie Mae   d. Governmental Accounting Standards Board

11. _____ is concerned with the provisions and use of accounting information to managers within organizations, to provide them with the basis to make informed business decisions that will allow them to be better equipped in their management and control functions.

In contrast to financial accountancy information, _____ information is:

- usually confidential and used by management, instead of publicly reported;
- forward-looking, instead of historical;
- pragmatically computed using extensive management information systems and internal controls, instead of complying with accounting standards.

This is because of the different emphasis: _____ information is used within an organization, typically for decision-making.

    a. Grenzplankostenrechnung   b. Governmental accounting
    c. Nonassurance services   d. Management Accounting

12. _____ refers to a business or organization attempting to acquire goods or services to accomplish the goals of the enterprise. Though there are several organizations that attempt to set standards in the _____ process, processes can vary greatly between organizations. Typically the word e;_____e; is not used interchangeably with the word e;procuremente;, since procurement typically includes Expediting, Supplier Quality, and Traffic and Logistics (T'L) in addition to _____.

    a. Supply chain   b. Free port
    c. Consignor   d. Purchasing

13. In business, _____, Overhead cost or _____ expense refers to an ongoing expense of operating a business. The term _____ is usually used to group expenses that are necessary to the continued functioning of the business, but do not directly generate profits.

_____ expenses are all costs on the income statement except for direct labor and direct materials.

   a. AIG
   c. ABC Television Network
   b. Intangible assets
   d. Overhead

14. _____ is a common concept in economics, and gives rise to derived concepts such as consumer debt. Generally _____ is defined by opposition to production. But the precise definition can vary because different schools of economists define production quite differently.

   a. Starving the beast
   c. Mitigating Control
   b. Consumption
   d. Yield

Chapter 10. Segmented Reporting, Investment Center Evaluation, and Transfer Pricing

1. A _____ is a fungible, negotiable instrument representing financial value. they are broadly categorized into debt securities (such as banknotes, bonds and debentures), and equity securities; e.g., common stocks. The company or other entity issuing the _____ is called the issuer.
   a. BMC Software, Inc.
   b. Tracking stock
   c. 3M Company
   d. Security

2. The U.S. _____ is an independent agency of the United States government which holds primary responsibility for enforcing the federal securities laws and regulating the securities industry, the nation's stock and options exchanges, and other electronic securities markets. The SEC was created by section 4 of the Securities Exchange Act of 1934 (now codified as 15 U.S.C. ÂÂ§ 78d and commonly referred to as the 1934 Act.)
   a. BMC Software, Inc.
   b. BNSF Railway
   c. Securities and Exchange Commission
   d. 3M Company

3. _____ can be regarded as an outcome of mental processes (cognitive process) leading to the selection of a course of action among several alternatives. Every _____ process produces a final choice. The output can be an action or an opinion of choice.
   a. BMC Software, Inc.
   b. BNSF Railway
   c. 3M Company
   d. Decision making

4. Just in Time could refer to the following:

   - _____, an inventory strategy that reduces in-process inventory
   - _____ compilation, a technique for improving the performance of bytecode-compiled programming systems

   a. Comparable
   b. Help desk and incident reporting auditing
   c. Fiscal
   d. Just-in-time

5. The _____ is a performance management tool which began as a concept for measuring whether the smaller-scale operational activities of a company are aligned with its larger-scale objectives in terms of vision and strategy.

   By focusing not only on financial outcomes but also on the operational, marketing and developmental inputs to these, the _____ helps provide a more comprehensive view of a business, which in turn helps organizations act in their best long-term interests. This tool is also being used to address business response to climate change and greenhouse gas emissions.

   a. Trustee
   b. Best practice
   c. Management by objectives
   d. Balanced Scorecard

6. _____ is an acronym for First In, First Out, an abstraction in ways of organizing and manipulation of data relative to time and prioritization. This expression describes the principle of a queue processing technique or servicing conflicting demands by ordering process by first-come, first-served (FCFS) behaviour: what comes in first is handled first, what comes in next waits until the first is finished, etc.

   Thus it is analogous to the behaviour of persons queueing (or 'standing in line', in common American parlance), where the persons leave the queue in the order they arrive, or waiting one's turn at a traffic control signal.

a. FIFO
c. Kanban
b. Risk management
d. Trademark

7. In financial accounting, a _____ is defined as an obligation of an entity arising from past transactions or events, the settlement of which may result in the transfer or use of assets, provision of services or other yielding of economic benefits in the future.
   a. Corporate governance
   c. Vested
   b. False Claims Act
   d. Liability

8. _____ is concerned with the provisions and use of accounting information to managers within organizations, to provide them with the basis to make informed business decisions that will allow them to be better equipped in their management and control functions.

In contrast to financial accountancy information, _____ information is:

- usually confidential and used by management, instead of publicly reported;
- forward-looking, instead of historical;
- pragmatically computed using extensive management information systems and internal controls, instead of complying with accounting standards.

This is because of the different emphasis: _____ information is used within an organization, typically for decision-making.

   a. Governmental accounting
   c. Grenzplankostenrechnung
   b. Management Accounting
   d. Nonassurance services

9. In economics, business, retail, and accounting, a _____ is the value of money that has been used up to produce something, and hence is not available for use anymore. In economics, a _____ is an alternative that is given up as a result of a decision. In business, the _____ may be one of acquisition, in which case the amount of money expended to acquire it is counted as _____.
   a. Cost of quality
   c. Cost allocation
   b. Prime cost
   d. Cost

10. _____ is systematic determination of merit, worth, and significance of something or someone using criteria against a set of standards. _____ often is used to characterize and appraise subjects of interest in a wide range of human enterprises, including the arts, criminal justice, foundations and non-profit organizations, government, health care, and other human services.

Depending on the topic of interest, there are professional groups which look to the quality and rigor of the _____ process.

   a. AIG
   c. AMEX
   b. ABC Television Network
   d. Evaluation

Chapter 10. Segmented Reporting, Investment Center Evaluation, and Transfer Pricing

11. An _____ is a classification used for business units within an enterprise. The essential element of an _____ is that it is treated as a unit which is measured against its use of capital, as opposed to a cost or profit center, which are measured against raw costs or profits.

The advantage of this form of measurement is that it tends to be more encompassing, since it accounts for all uses of capital.

a. ABC Television Network
c. AMEX
b. AIG
d. Investment center

12. _____s are parts of a corporation that directly add to its profit.

A _____ manager is held accountable for both revenues, and costs (expenses), and therefore, profits. What this means in terms of managerial responsibilities is that the manager has to drive the sales revenue generating activities which leads to cash inflows and at the same time control the cost (cash outflows) causing activities.

a. Contribution margin
c. Cost driver
b. Profit center
d. Cost management

13. Total _____ is a method of Accounting cost which entails the full cost of manufacturing or providing a service. This includes not just the costs of materials and labour, but also of all manufacturing overheads (whether e;fixede; or e;variablee;.) One of the main reasons for absorbing overheads into the cost of units is for inventory valuation purposes.

a. ABC Television Network
c. Absorption costing
b. AMEX
d. AIG

14. _____ is a company's financial statement that indicates how the revenue is transformed into the net income The purpose of the _____ is to show managers and investors whether the company made or lost money during the period being reported.

The important thing to remember about an _____ is that it represents a period of time.

a. ABC Television Network
c. AMEX
b. AIG
d. Income statement

15. An _____ allows a company to provide a monetary value for items that make up their inventory. Inventories are usually the largest current asset of a business, and proper measurement of them is necessary to assure accurate financial statements. If inventory is not properly measured, expenses and revenues cannot be properly matched and a company could make poor business decisions.

a. AIG
c. ABC Television Network
b. Inventory valuation
d. AMEX

16. In finance, _____ is the process of estimating the potential market value of a financial asset or liability. They can be done on assets (for example, investments in marketable securities such as stocks, options, business enterprises, or intangible assets such as patents and trademarks) or on liabilities (e.g., Bonds issued by a company.) A _____ is required in many contexts including investment analysis, capital budgeting, merger and acquisition transactions, financial reporting, taxable events to determine the proper tax liability, and in litigation.

a. Daybook	b. Valuation
c. Disclosure	d. Vyborg Appeal

17. A _____ is the pinnacle activity involved in selling products or services in return for money or other compensation. It is an act of completion of a commercial activity.

A _____ is completed by the seller, the owner of the goods.

a. Maturity	b. Tertiary sector of economy
c. High yield stock	d. Sale

18. The _____ is a private, not-for-profit organization whose primary purpose is to develop generally accepted accounting principles (GAAP) within the United States in the public's interest. The Securities and Exchange Commission (SEC) designated the _____ as the organization responsible for setting accounting standards for public companies in the U.S. It was created in 1973, replacing the Accounting Principles Board and the Committee on Accounting Procedure of the American Institute of Certified Public Accountants. The _____'s mission is 'to establish and improve standards of financial accounting and reporting for the guidance and education of the public, including issuers, auditors, and users of financial information.'

The _____ is not a governmental body.

a. Financial Accounting Standards Board	b. Governmental Accounting Standards Board
c. Fannie Mae	d. Public company

19. In business, _____, Overhead cost or _____ expense refers to an ongoing expense of operating a business. The term _____ is usually used to group expenses that are necessary to the continued functioning of the business, but do not directly generate profits.

_____ expenses are all costs on the income statement except for direct labor and direct materials.

a. AIG	b. Overhead
c. Intangible assets	d. ABC Television Network

20. In accounting, _____ has a very specific meaning. It is an outflow of cash or other valuable assets from a person or company to another person or company. This outflow of cash is generally one side of a trade for products or services that have equal or better current or future value to the buyer than to the seller.

a. AIG	b. AMEX
c. ABC Television Network	d. Expense

21. In business and accounting, _____ are everything of value that is owned by a person or company. It is a claim on the property your income of a borrower. The balance sheet of a firm records the monetary value of the _____ owned by the firm.

a. Accrual basis accounting	b. Earnings before interest, taxes, depreciation and amortization
c. Accounts receivable	d. Assets

Chapter 10. Segmented Reporting, Investment Center Evaluation, and Transfer Pricing

22. _____ is the difference between operating revenues and operating expenses, but it is also sometimes used as a synonym for EBIT and operating profit. This is true if the firm has no non-_____.

A professional investor contemplating a change to the capital structure of a firm first evaluates a firm's fundamental earnings potential (reflected by Earnings Before Interest, Taxes, Depreciation and Amortization EBITDA and EBIT), and then determines the optimal use of debt vs. equity.

a. ABC Television Network
b. AMEX
c. AIG
d. Operating income

23. In finance, _____ also known as return on investment, rate of profit or sometimes just return, is the ratio of money gained or lost on an investment relative to the amount of money invested. The amount of money gained or lost may be referred to as interest, profit/loss, gain/loss, or net income/loss. The money invested may be referred to as the asset, capital, principal, or the cost basis of the investment.

a. Theoretical ex-rights price
b. Capital employed
c. Debt to capital ratio
d. Rate of return

24. In corporate finance, _____ or _____ is an estimate of true economic profit after making corrective adjustments to GAAP accounting, including deducting the opportunity cost of equity capital. _____ can be measured as Net Operating Profit After Taxes(or NOPAT) less the money cost of capital. _____ is similar in nature to that of calculating another financial performance measure - Residual Income , however, there are a few complexities involved with coming up with the elements for calculating _____ over RI such as the myriad adjustments that might be made to NOPAT before it is suitable for the formula below.

a. Economic value added
b. Internal control
c. International Monetary Fund
d. Outsourcing

25. _____ refers to the additional value of a commodity over the cost of commodities used to produce it from the previous stage of production. An example is the price of gasoline at the pump over the price of the oil in it. In national accounts used in macroeconomics, it refers to the contribution of the factors of production, i.e., land, labor, and capital goods, to raising the value of a product and corresponds to the incomes received by the owners of these factors.

a. 3M Company
b. Minimum wage
c. Supply-side economics
d. Value added

26. _____ is one of the four Ps of the marketing mix. The other three aspects are product, promotion, and place. It is also a key variable in microeconomic price allocation theory.

a. Cost-plus pricing
b. Price
c. Pricing
d. Target costing

27. _____ refers to the pricing of contributions (assets, tangible and intangible, services, and funds) transferred within an organization. For example, goods from the production division may be sold to the marketing division, or goods from a parent company may be sold to a foreign subsidiary. Since the prices are set within an organization (i.e. controlled), the typical market mechanisms that establish prices for such transactions between third parties may not apply.

a. Price
b. Pricing
c. Transfer pricing
d. Transactional Net Margin Method

Chapter 10. Segmented Reporting, Investment Center Evaluation, and Transfer Pricing

28. A _____ is an entity formed between two or more parties to undertake economic activity together. The parties agree to create a new entity by both contributing equity, and they then share in the revenues, expenses, and control of the enterprise. The venture can be for one specific project only, or a continuing business relationship such as the Fuji Xerox _____.
   a. Joint venture
   b. Pre-emption right
   c. Chief Financial Officers Act of 1990
   d. Fraud Enforcement and Recovery Act

29. _____ or economic opportunity loss is the value of the next best alternative foregone as the result of making a decision. _____ analysis is an important part of a company's decision-making processes but is not treated as an actual cost in any financial statement. The next best thing that a person can engage in is referred to as the _____ of doing the best thing and ignoring the next best thing to be done.
   a. Inflation
   b. ABC Television Network
   c. Opportunity cost
   d. AIG

30. _____ in economics and business is the result of an exchange and from that trade we assign a numerical monetary value to a good, service or asset. If Alice trades Bob 4 apples for an orange, the _____ of an orange is 4 apples. Inversely, the _____ of an apple is 1/4 oranges.
   a. Price discrimination
   b. Discounts and allowances
   c. Transactional Net Margin Method
   d. Price

31. A _____ is any one of a variety of different systems, institutions, procedures, social relations and infrastructures whereby persons trade, and goods and services are exchanged, forming part of the economy. It is an arrangement that allows buyers and sellers to exchange things. _____s vary in size, range, geographic scale, location, types and variety of human communities, as well as the types of goods and services traded.
   a. Market Failure
   b. Recession
   c. Perfect competition
   d. Market

32. _____ is an economic concept with commonplace familiarity. It is the price that a good or service is offered at, or will fetch, in the marketplace. It is of interest mainly in the study of microeconomics.
   a. Transfer agent
   b. Spot rate
   c. Financial instruments
   d. Market price

Chapter 11. Cost-Volume-Profit Analysis: A Managerial Planning Tool 57

1. In financial accounting, a _____ is defined as an obligation of an entity arising from past transactions or events, the settlement of which may result in the transfer or use of assets, provision of services or other yielding of economic benefits in the future.
   - a. Corporate governance
   - b. Vested
   - c. Liability
   - d. False Claims Act

2. _____, in managerial economics is a form of cost accounting. It is a simplified model, useful for elementary instruction and for short-run decisions.

Cost-volume-profit (CVP) analysis expands the use of information provided by breakeven analysis.

   - a. Cost accounting
   - b. Cost-volume-profit analysis
   - c. Fixed costs
   - d. Cost of quality

3. In economics ' business, specifically cost accounting, the _____ is the point at which cost or expenses and revenue are equal: there is no net loss or gain, and one has 'broken even'. A profit or a loss has not been made, although opportunity costs have been paid, and capital has received the risk-adjusted, expected return.

For example, if the business sells less than 200 tables each month, it will make a loss, if it sells more, it will be a profit.

   - a. Break-even point
   - b. BMC Software, Inc.
   - c. Defined benefit pension plan
   - d. 3M Company

4. _____ is the difference between operating revenues and operating expenses, but it is also sometimes used as a synonym for EBIT and operating profit. This is true if the firm has no non-_____.

A professional investor contemplating a change to the capital structure of a firm first evaluates a firm's fundamental earnings potential (reflected by Earnings Before Interest, Taxes, Depreciation and Amortization EBITDA and EBIT), and then determines the optimal use of debt vs. equity.

   - a. AIG
   - b. AMEX
   - c. ABC Television Network
   - d. Operating income

5. A _____ is an entity formed between two or more parties to undertake economic activity together. The parties agree to create a new entity by both contributing equity, and they then share in the revenues, expenses, and control of the enterprise. The venture can be for one specific project only, or a continuing business relationship such as the Fuji Xerox _____.
   - a. Fraud Enforcement and Recovery Act
   - b. Joint venture
   - c. Chief Financial Officers Act of 1990
   - d. Pre-emption right

6. _____ is equal to the income that a firm has after subtracting costs and expenses from the total revenue. _____ can be distributed among holders of common stock as a dividend or held by the firm as retained earnings.

The items deducted will typically include tax expense, financing expense (interest expense), and minority interest. Likewise, preferred stock dividends will be subtracted too, though they are not an expense.

Chapter 11. Cost-Volume-Profit Analysis: A Managerial Planning Tool

a. Long-term liabilities
b. Matching principle
c. Generally accepted accounting principles
d. Net income

7. In cost-volume-profit analysis, a form of management accounting, _____ is the marginal profit per unit sale. It is a useful quantity in carrying out various calculations, and can be used as a measure of operating leverage.

The Total _____ is Total Revenue (TR, or Sales) minus Total Variable Cost (TVC):

Tcontribution margin = TR − TVC

The Unit _____ (C) is Unit Revenue (Price, P) minus Unit Variable Cost (V):

C = P − V

The _____ Ratio is the percentage of Contribution over Total Revenue, which can be calculated from the unit contribution over unit price or total contribution over Total Revenue:

$$\frac{C}{P} = \frac{P-V}{P} = \frac{\text{Unit Contribution Margin}}{\text{Price}} = \frac{\text{Total Contribution Margin}}{\text{Total Revenue}}$$

For instance, if the price is $10 and the unit variable cost is $2, then the unit _____ is $8, and the _____ ratio is $8/$10 = 80%.

a. Profit center
b. Contribution margin
c. Cost management
d. Factory overhead

8. A _____ is the pinnacle activity involved in selling products or services in return for money or other compensation. It is an act of completion of a commercial activity.

A _____ is completed by the seller, the owner of the goods.

a. High yield stock
b. Maturity
c. Tertiary sector of economy
d. Sale

9. _____ is an acronym for First In, First Out, an abstraction in ways of organizing and manipulation of data relative to time and prioritization. This expression describes the principle of a queue processing technique or servicing conflicting demands by ordering process by first-come, first-served (FCFS) behaviour: what comes in first is handled first, what comes in next waits until the first is finished, etc.

Thus it is analogous to the behaviour of persons queueing (or 'standing in line', in common American parlance), where the persons leave the queue in the order they arrive, or waiting one's turn at a traffic control signal.

a. Risk management
b. Kanban
c. Trademark
d. FIFO

Chapter 11. Cost-Volume-Profit Analysis: A Managerial Planning Tool

10. In economics, business, retail, and accounting, a _____ is the value of money that has been used up to produce something, and hence is not available for use anymore. In economics, a _____ is an alternative that is given up as a result of a decision. In business, the _____ may be one of acquisition, in which case the amount of money expended to acquire it is counted as _____.
    a. Cost allocation
    b. Cost of quality
    c. Cost
    d. Prime cost

11. _____s are expenses that change in proportion to the activity of a business. In other words, _____ is the sum of marginal costs. It can also be considered normal costs.
    a. Fixed costs
    b. Quality costs
    c. Cost accounting
    d. Variable cost

12. In accounting, _____ has a very specific meaning. It is an outflow of cash or other valuable assets from a person or company to another person or company. This outflow of cash is generally one side of a trade for products or services that have equal or better current or future value to the buyer than to the seller.
    a. AIG
    b. ABC Television Network
    c. AMEX
    d. Expense

13. The _____ is a United States law enacted in 1993. It is one of a series of laws designed to improve government project management. The GPRA requires agencies to engage in project management tasks such as setting goals, measuring results, and reporting their progress.
    a. Government Performance and Results Act
    b. BMC Software, Inc.
    c. 3M Company
    d. BNSF Railway

14. The _____ is a performance management tool which began as a concept for measuring whether the smaller-scale operational activities of a company are aligned with its larger-scale objectives in terms of vision and strategy.

By focusing not only on financial outcomes but also on the operational, marketing and developmental inputs to these, the _____ helps provide a more comprehensive view of a business, which in turn helps organizations act in their best long-term interests. This tool is also being used to address business response to climate change and greenhouse gas emissions.

    a. Management by objectives
    b. Trustee
    c. Best practice
    d. Balanced Scorecard

15. _____ is one of the four Ps of the marketing mix. The other three aspects are product, promotion, and place. It is also a key variable in microeconomic price allocation theory.
    a. Price
    b. Target costing
    c. Cost-plus pricing
    d. Pricing

16. _____ in economics refers to metrics and measures of output from production processes, per unit of input. Labor _____, for example, is typically measured as a ratio of output per labor-hour, an input. _____ may be conceived of as a metrics of the technical or engineering efficiency of production.
    a. Cellular manufacturing
    b. Deming Prize
    c. Value engineering
    d. Productivity

Chapter 11. Cost-Volume-Profit Analysis: A Managerial Planning Tool

17. The concept of _____ is a means to quantify the total cost of quality-related efforts and deficiencies. It was first described by Armand V. Feigenbaum in a 1956 Harvard Business Review article.

Prior to its introduction, the general perception was that higher quality requires higher costs, either by buying better materials or machines or by hiring more labor.

a. Marginal cost
c. Cost allocation

b. Variable cost
d. Quality costs

18. _____ is concerned with the provisions and use of accounting information to managers within organizations, to provide them with the basis to make informed business decisions that will allow them to be better equipped in their management and control functions.

In contrast to financial accountancy information, _____ information is:

- usually confidential and used by management, instead of publicly reported;
- forward-looking, instead of historical;
- pragmatically computed using extensive management information systems and internal controls, instead of complying with accounting standards.

This is because of the different emphasis: _____ information is used within an organization, typically for decision-making.

a. Management Accounting
c. Nonassurance services

b. Grenzplankostenrechnung
d. Governmental accounting

19. The _____ is a measure of how revenue growth translates into growth in operating income. It is a measure of leverage, and of how risky (volatile) a company's operating income is.

There are various measures of _____, which can be interpreted analogously to financial leverage.

a. AlphaIC
c. Upside potential ratio

b. Information ratio
d. Operating leverage

20. _____ is a concept that denotes the precise probability of specific eventualities. Technically, the notion of _____ is independent from the notion of value and, as such, eventualities may have both beneficial and adverse consequences. However, in general usage the convention is to focus only on potential negative impact to some characteristic of value that may arise from a future event.

a. Discounting
c. Risk

b. Risk adjusted return on capital
d. Discount factor

21. A _____ is a fungible, negotiable instrument representing financial value. they are broadly categorized into debt securities (such as banknotes, bonds and debentures), and equity securities; e.g., common stocks. The company or other entity issuing the _____ is called the issuer.

Chapter 11. Cost-Volume-Profit Analysis: A Managerial Planning Tool

a. 3M Company
c. BMC Software, Inc.
b. Tracking stock
d. Security

22. The U.S. _____ is an independent agency of the United States government which holds primary responsibility for enforcing the federal securities laws and regulating the securities industry, the nation's stock and options exchanges, and other electronic securities markets. The SEC was created by section 4 of the Securities Exchange Act of 1934 (now codified as 15 U.S.C. ÂÂ§ 78d and commonly referred to as the 1934 Act.)

a. BNSF Railway
c. 3M Company
b. Securities and Exchange Commission
d. BMC Software, Inc.

23. _____ is the study of how the variation (uncertainty) in the output of a mathematical model can be apportioned, qualitatively or quantitatively, to different sources of variation in the input of a model .

In more general terms uncertainty and sensitivity analyses investigate the robustness of a study when the study includes some form of mathematical modelling. While uncertainty analysis studies the overall uncertainty in the conclusions of the study, _____ tries to identify what source of uncertainty weights more on the study's conclusions.

a. Sensitivity analysis
c. Kaizen
b. Time to market
d. Free cash flow

24. _____ is a costing model that identifies activities in an organization and assigns the cost of each activity resource to all products and services according to the actual consumption by each: it assigns more indirect costs (overhead) into direct costs.

In this way an organization can establish the true cost of its individual products and services for the purposes of identifying and eliminating those which are unprofitable and lowering the prices of those which are overpriced.

In a business organization, the ABC methodology assigns an organization's resource costs through activities to the products and services provided to its customers.

a. Activity-based costing
c. Indirect costs
b. Activity-based management
d. ABC Television Network

25. Just in Time could refer to the following:

- _____, an inventory strategy that reduces in-process inventory
- _____ compilation, a technique for improving the performance of bytecode-compiled programming systems

a. Just-in-time
c. Comparable
b. Help desk and incident reporting auditing
d. Fiscal

Chapter 12. Tactical Decision Making

1. An _____ is a practitioner of accountancy, which is the measurement, disclosure or provision of assurance about financial information that helps managers, investors, tax authorities and other decision makers make resource allocation decisions.

The word '_____' is derived from the French 'Compter' which took its origin from the Latin 'Computare'. The word was formerly written in English as 'Accomptant', but in process of time the word, which was always pronounced by dropping the 'p', became gradually changed both in pronunciation and in orthography to its present form.

   a. AIG
   b. AMEX
   c. ABC Television Network
   d. Accountant

2. The _____ is a professional organization headquartered in Montvale, New Jersey consisting of over 70,000 members worldwide. The IMA is dedicated to advancing the role of the management accountant and financial manager within the business organization, and provides relevant professional certification.

The IMA awards the Certified Management Accountant (CMA) designation in the United States.

   a. American Accounting Association
   b. International Accounting Standards Committee
   c. Emerging technologies
   d. Institute of Management Accountants

3. _____ is concerned with the provisions and use of accounting information to managers within organizations, to provide them with the basis to make informed business decisions that will allow them to be better equipped in their management and control functions.

In contrast to financial accountancy information, _____ information is:

   - usually confidential and used by management, instead of publicly reported;
   - forward-looking, instead of historical;
   - pragmatically computed using extensive management information systems and internal controls, instead of complying with accounting standards.

This is because of the different emphasis: _____ information is used within an organization, typically for decision-making.

   a. Grenzplankostenrechnung
   b. Nonassurance services
   c. Governmental accounting
   d. Management accounting

4. _____ can be regarded as an outcome of mental processes (cognitive process) leading to the selection of a course of action among several alternatives. Every _____ process produces a final choice. The output can be an action or an opinion of choice.

   a. BMC Software, Inc.
   b. BNSF Railway
   c. 3M Company
   d. Decision making

Chapter 12. Tactical Decision Making

5. In economics, _____ or _____ goods or real _____ refers to factors of production used to create goods or services that are not themselves significantly consumed (though they may depreciate) in the production process. _____ goods may be acquired with money or financial _____. In finance and accounting, _____ generally refers to financial wealth, especially that used to start or maintain a business.
   a. Screening
   b. Capital
   c. Vyborg Appeal
   d. Disclosure

6. _____ are made by investors and investment managers.

Investors commonly perform investment analysis by making use of fundamental analysis, technical analysis and gut feel.

_____ are often supported by decision tools.

   a. ABC Television Network
   b. Incremental capital-output ratio
   c. AIG
   d. Investment decisions

7. In economics, business, retail, and accounting, a _____ is the value of money that has been used up to produce something, and hence is not available for use anymore. In economics, a _____ is an alternative that is given up as a result of a decision. In business, the _____ may be one of acquisition, in which case the amount of money expended to acquire it is counted as _____.
   a. Cost allocation
   b. Cost of quality
   c. Prime cost
   d. Cost

8. The _____ is a private, not-for-profit organization whose primary purpose is to develop generally accepted accounting principles (GAAP) within the United States in the public's interest. The Securities and Exchange Commission (SEC) designated the _____ as the organization responsible for setting accounting standards for public companies in the U.S. It was created in 1973, replacing the Accounting Principles Board and the Committee on Accounting Procedure of the American Institute of Certified Public Accountants. The _____'s mission is 'to establish and improve standards of financial accounting and reporting for the guidance and education of the public, including issuers, auditors, and users of financial information.'

The _____ is not a governmental body.

   a. Financial Accounting Standards Board
   b. Fannie Mae
   c. Governmental Accounting Standards Board
   d. Public company

9. In financial accounting, a _____ is defined as an obligation of an entity arising from past transactions or events, the settlement of which may result in the transfer or use of assets, provision of services or other yielding of economic benefits in the future.
   a. Corporate governance
   b. False Claims Act
   c. Vested
   d. Liability

10. _____ is a concept related to lean and just-in-time (JIT) production. The Japanese word _____ is a common everyday term meaning 'signboard' or 'billboard' and utterly lacks the specialized meaning that this loanword has acquired in English. According to Taiichi Ohno, the man credited with developing JIT, _____ is a means through which JIT is achieved.
   a. Risk management
   b. Trademark
   c. FIFO
   d. Kanban

11. A _____ is a fungible, negotiable instrument representing financial value. they are broadly categorized into debt securities (such as banknotes, bonds and debentures), and equity securities; e.g., common stocks. The company or other entity issuing the _____ is called the issuer.
   a. Tracking stock
   b. Security
   c. BMC Software, Inc.
   d. 3M Company

12. The U.S. _____ is an independent agency of the United States government which holds primary responsibility for enforcing the federal securities laws and regulating the securities industry, the nation's stock and options exchanges, and other electronic securities markets. The SEC was created by section 4 of the Securities Exchange Act of 1934 (now codified as 15 U.S.C. ÂÂ§ 78d and commonly referred to as the 1934 Act.)
   a. BNSF Railway
   b. 3M Company
   c. BMC Software, Inc.
   d. Securities and Exchange Commission

13. _____ is systematic determination of merit, worth, and significance of something or someone using criteria against a set of standards. _____ often is used to characterize and appraise subjects of interest in a wide range of human enterprises, including the arts, criminal justice, foundations and non-profit organizations, government, health care, and other human services.

Depending on the topic of interest, there are professional groups which look to the quality and rigor of the _____ process.

   a. ABC Television Network
   b. AMEX
   c. Evaluation
   d. AIG

14. An _____ is a classification used for business units within an enterprise. The essential element of an _____ is that it is treated as a unit which is measured against its use of capital, as opposed to a cost or profit center, which are measured against raw costs or profits.

The advantage of this form of measurement is that it tends to be more encompassing, since it accounts for all uses of capital.

   a. AIG
   b. ABC Television Network
   c. AMEX
   d. Investment center

15. _____ is one of the four Ps of the marketing mix. The other three aspects are product, promotion, and place. It is also a key variable in microeconomic price allocation theory.
   a. Price
   b. Target costing
   c. Cost-plus pricing
   d. Pricing

16. _____ refers to a business or organization attempting to acquire goods or services to accomplish the goals of the enterprise. Though there are several organizations that attempt to set standards in the _____ process, processes can vary greatly between organizations. Typically the word e;_____e; is not used interchangeably with the word e;procuremente;, since procurement typically includes Expediting, Supplier Quality, and Traffic and Logistics (T'L) in addition to _____.
- a. Free port
- b. Supply chain
- c. Consignor
- d. Purchasing

17. _____ refers to the pricing of contributions (assets, tangible and intangible, services, and funds) transferred within an organization. For example, goods from the production division may be sold to the marketing division, or goods from a parent company may be sold to a foreign subsidiary. Since the prices are set within an organization (i.e. controlled), the typical market mechanisms that establish prices for such transactions between third parties may not apply.
- a. Price
- b. Transactional Net Margin Method
- c. Pricing
- d. Transfer pricing

18. The _____ is a performance management tool which began as a concept for measuring whether the smaller-scale operational activities of a company are aligned with its larger-scale objectives in terms of vision and strategy.

By focusing not only on financial outcomes but also on the operational, marketing and developmental inputs to these, the _____ helps provide a more comprehensive view of a business, which in turn helps organizations act in their best long-term interests. This tool is also being used to address business response to climate change and greenhouse gas emissions.

- a. Management by objectives
- b. Trustee
- c. Best practice
- d. Balanced Scorecard

19. _____ in economics refers to metrics and measures of output from production processes, per unit of input. Labor _____, for example, is typically measured as a ratio of output per labor-hour, an input. _____ may be conceived of as a metrics of the technical or engineering efficiency of production.
- a. Cellular manufacturing
- b. Value engineering
- c. Productivity
- d. Deming Prize

20. The concept of _____ is a means to quantify the total cost of quality-related efforts and deficiencies. It was first described by Armand V. Feigenbaum in a 1956 Harvard Business Review article.

Prior to its introduction, the general perception was that higher quality requires higher costs, either by buying better materials or machines or by hiring more labor.

- a. Cost allocation
- b. Variable cost
- c. Marginal cost
- d. Quality costs

21. In mathematics, _____ is a technique for optimization of a linear objective function, subject to linear equality and linear inequality constraints. Informally, _____ determines the way to achieve the best outcome (such as maximum profit or lowest cost) in a given mathematical model and given some list of requirements represented as linear equations.

More formally, given a polytope (for example, a polygon or a polyhedron), and a real-valued affine function

$$f(x_1, x_2, \ldots, x_n) = c_1 x_1 + c_2 x_2 + \cdots + c_n x_n + d$$

defined on this polytope, a _____ method will find a point in the polytope where this function has the smallest (or largest) value.

a. BNSF Railway
b. BMC Software, Inc.
c. Linear programming
d. 3M Company

22. _____ is the difference between the cost of a good or service and its selling price. A _____ is added on to the total cost incurred by the producer of a good or service in order to create a profit. The total cost reflects the total amount of both fixed and variable expenses to produce and distribute a product.
a. Statements of Financial Accounting Standards No. 133, Accounting for Derivative Instruments and Hedging Activities
b. Merck ' Co., Inc.
c. Markup
d. Corporate Bond

23. _____ is accounting for the lean enterprise. It seeks to move from traditional cost accounting to a system that measures and motivates good business practices in the lean enterprise.

Lean manufacturing methods were first introduced into the United States and other Western countries in the 1980's; primarily by the Toyota companies.

a. 3M Company
b. BNSF Railway
c. BMC Software, Inc.
d. Lean accounting

24. _____ is a pricing method used by firms. It is defined as 'a cost management tool for reducing the overall cost of a product over its entire life-cycle with the help of production, engineering, research and design'. A target cost is the maximum amount of cost that can be incurred on a product and with it the firm can still earn the required profit margin from that product at a particular selling price.
a. Pricing
b. Penetration pricing
c. Discounts and allowances
d. Target costing

25. _____ is the practice of selling a product or service at a very low price, intending to drive competitors out of the market, or create barriers to entry for potential new competitors. If competitors or potential competitors cannot sustain equal or lower prices without losing money, they go out of business or choose not to enter the business. The predatory merchant then has fewer competitors or is even a de facto monopoly, and can then raise prices above what the market would otherwise bear.
a. Predatory pricing
b. 3M Company
c. BNSF Railway
d. BMC Software, Inc.

26. The _____ of 1936 (or Anti-Price Discrimination Act, 15 U.S.C. § 13) is a United States federal law that prohibits what were considered, at the time of passage, to be anticompetitive practices by producers, specifically price discrimination. It grew out of practices in which chain stores were allowed to purchase goods at lower prices than other retailers.

a. Lien
b. Limited liability
c. Robinson-Patman Act
d. Consumer protection laws

27. _____ in economics and business is the result of an exchange and from that trade we assign a numerical monetary value to a good, service or asset. If Alice trades Bob 4 apples for an orange, the _____ of an orange is 4 apples. Inversely, the _____ of an apple is 1/4 oranges.
   a. Price discrimination
   b. Price
   c. Transactional Net Margin Method
   d. Discounts and allowances

28. _____ exists when sales of identical goods or services are transacted at different prices from the same provider. In a theoretical market with perfect information, no transaction costs or prohibition on secondary exchange (or re-selling) to prevent arbitrage, _____ can only be a feature of monopoly and oligopoly markets, where market power can be exercised. Otherwise, the moment the seller tries to sell the same good at different prices, the buyer at the lower price can arbitrage by selling to the consumer buying at the higher price but with a tiny discount.
   a. Transactional Net Margin Method
   b. Price
   c. Resale price maintenance
   d. Price discrimination

Chapter 13. Capital Investment Decisions

1. In economics, _____ or _____ goods or real _____ refers to factors of production used to create goods or services that are not themselves significantly consumed (though they may depreciate) in the production process. _____ goods may be acquired with money or financial _____. In finance and accounting, _____ generally refers to financial wealth, especially that used to start or maintain a business.
   a. Disclosure
   b. Screening
   c. Capital
   d. Vyborg Appeal

2. _____ are made by investors and investment managers.

   Investors commonly perform investment analysis by making use of fundamental analysis, technical analysis and gut feel.

   _____ are often supported by decision tools.

   a. Incremental capital-output ratio
   b. AIG
   c. Investment decisions
   d. ABC Television Network

3. Project _____: The project _____ is a prediction of the costs associated with a particular company project. These costs include labor, materials, and other related expenses. The project _____ is often broken down into specific tasks, with task _____s assigned to each.
   a. BNSF Railway
   b. Budget
   c. BMC Software, Inc.
   d. 3M Company

4. _____ is the planning process used to determine whether a firm's long term investments such as new machinery, replacement machinery, new plants, new products, and research development projects are worth pursuing. It is budget for major capital, or investment, expenditures.

   Many formal methods are used in _____, including the techniques such as

   - Net present value
   - Profitability index
   - Internal rate of return
   - Modified Internal Rate of Return
   - Equivalent annuity

   These methods use the incremental cash flows from each potential investment, or project. Techniques based on accounting earnings and accounting rules are sometimes used - though economists consider this to be improper - such as the accounting rate of return, and 'return on investment.' Simplified and hybrid methods are used as well, such as payback period and discounted payback period.

   a. Gross profit
   b. Preferred stock
   c. Cash flow
   d. Capital budgeting

5. A _____ is an entity formed between two or more parties to undertake economic activity together. The parties agree to create a new entity by both contributing equity, and they then share in the revenues, expenses, and control of the enterprise. The venture can be for one specific project only, or a continuing business relationship such as the Fuji Xerox _____.

a. Chief Financial Officers Act of 1990
b. Fraud Enforcement and Recovery Act
c. Pre-emption right
d. Joint venture

6. There are many _____ entity defined in the legal systems of various countries. These include corporations, partnerships, sole traders and other specialized types of organization. Some of these types are listed below, by country.
a. Bond indenture
b. Staple right
c. Hospital Survey and Construction Act
d. Types of Business

7. _____ is a financial mechanism in which a debtor obtains the right to delay payments to a creditor, for a defined period of time, in exchange for a charge or fee. Essentially, the party that owes money in the present purchases the right to delay the payment until some future date. The discount, or charge, is simply the difference between the original amount owed in the present and the amount that has to be paid in the future to settle the debt.
a. Risk adjusted return on capital
b. Risk aversion
c. Discount factor
d. Discounting

8. _____ in business and economics refers to the period of time required for the return on an investment to 'repay' the sum of the original investment. For example, a $1000 investment which returned $500 per year would have a two year _____. It intuitively measures how long something takes to 'pay for itself.' Shorter _____s are obviously preferable to longer _____s (all else being equal.)
a. Payback period
b. Fair market value
c. Segregated portfolio company
d. Net worth

9. An _____ is a practitioner of accountancy, which is the measurement, disclosure or provision of assurance about financial information that helps managers, investors, tax authorities and other decision makers make resource allocation decisions.

The word '_____' is derived from the French 'Compter' which took its origin from the Latin 'Computare'. The word was formerly written in English as 'Accomptant', but in process of time the word, which was always pronounced by dropping the 'p', became gradually changed both in pronunciation and in orthography to its present form.

a. ABC Television Network
b. AIG
c. AMEX
d. Accountant

10. The _____ is a professional organization headquartered in Montvale, New Jersey consisting of over 70,000 members worldwide. The IMA is dedicated to advancing the role of the management accountant and financial manager within the business organization, and provides relevant professional certification.

The IMA awards the Certified Management Accountant (CMA) designation in the United States.

a. International Accounting Standards Committee
b. Institute of Management Accountants
c. American Accounting Association
d. Emerging technologies

11. _____ is concerned with the provisions and use of accounting information to managers within organizations, to provide them with the basis to make informed business decisions that will allow them to be better equipped in their management and control functions.

In contrast to financial accountancy information, _____ information is:

- usually confidential and used by management, instead of publicly reported;
- forward-looking, instead of historical;
- pragmatically computed using extensive management information systems and internal controls, instead of complying with accounting standards.

This is because of the different emphasis: _____ information is used within an organization, typically for decision-making.

a. Nonassurance services
b. Governmental accounting
c. Management accounting
d. Grenzplankostenrechnung

12. _____ is the balance of the amounts of cash being received and paid by a business during a defined period of time, sometimes tied to a specific project. Measurement of _____ can be used

- to evaluate the state or performance of a business or project.
- to determine problems with liquidity. Being profitable does not necessarily mean being liquid. A company can fail because of a shortage of cash, even while profitable.
- to project rate of returns. The time of _____s into and out of projects are used as inputs to financial models such as internal rate of return, and net present value.
- to examine income or growth of a business when it is believed that accrual accounting concepts do not represent economic realities. Alternately, _____ can be used to 'validate' the net income generated by accrual accounting.

_____ as a generic term may be used differently depending on context, and certain _____ definitions may be adapted by analysts and users for their own uses. Common terms include operating _____ and free _____.

a. Controlling interest
b. Cash flow
c. Flow-through entity
d. Commercial paper

13. In finance, the _____ approach describes a method of valuing a project, company, or asset using the concepts of the time value of money. All future cash flows are estimated and discounted to give their present values. The discount rate used is generally the appropriate WACC, that reflects the risk of the cashflows.

a. Net present value
b. Future value
c. 3M Company
d. Discounted cash flow

14. An _____ is a term used in behavioral economics to describe those types of behaviors that impose costs on a person in the long-run that are not taken into account when making decisions in the present. Classical Economics discourages government from creating legislation that targets internalities, because it is assumed that the consumer takes these personal costs into account when paying for the good that causes the _____. For example, cigarettes should be taxed because of the negative consumption externalities that they impose, such as second-hand smoke, not because the smoker harms him or herself by smoking.

a. Inventory turnover ratio
b. Operating budget
c. Internality
d. Authorised capital

15. The _____ is a capital budgeting metric used by firms to decide whether they should make investments. It is also called discounted cash flow rate of return (DCFROR) or rate of return (ROR.) It is an indicator of the efficiency or quality of an investment, as opposed to net present value (NPV), which indicates value or magnitude.
   a. AIG
   b. ABC Television Network
   c. AMEX
   d. Internal rate of return

16. _____ or net present worth (NPW) is defined as the total present value (PV) of a time series of cash flows. It is a standard method for using the time value of money to appraise long-term projects. Used for capital budgeting, and widely throughout economics, it measures the excess or shortfall of cash flows, in present value terms, once financing charges are met.
   a. Future value
   b. Present value
   c. 3M Company
   d. Net present value

17. _____ is the value on a given date of a future payment or series of future payments, discounted to reflect the time value of money and other factors such as investment risk. _____ calculations are widely used in business and economics to provide a means to compare cash flows at different times on a meaningful 'like to like' basis.

The most commonly applied model of the time value of money is compound interest.

   a. 3M Company
   b. Present value
   c. Future value
   d. Net present value

18. In finance, _____ also known as return on investment, rate of profit or sometimes just return, is the ratio of money gained or lost on an investment relative to the amount of money invested. The amount of money gained or lost may be referred to as interest, profit/loss, gain/loss, or net income/loss. The money invested may be referred to as the asset, capital, principal, or the cost basis of the investment.
   a. Theoretical ex-rights price
   b. Rate of return
   c. Capital employed
   d. Debt to capital ratio

19. In financial accounting, a _____ is defined as an obligation of an entity arising from past transactions or events, the settlement of which may result in the transfer or use of assets, provision of services or other yielding of economic benefits in the future.
   a. Corporate governance
   b. False Claims Act
   c. Liability
   d. Vested

20. In economics, business, retail, and accounting, a _____ is the value of money that has been used up to produce something, and hence is not available for use anymore. In economics, a _____ is an alternative that is given up as a result of a decision. In business, the _____ may be one of acquisition, in which case the amount of money expended to acquire it is counted as _____.
   a. Cost of quality
   b. Prime cost
   c. Cost allocation
   d. Cost

21. The _____ is an expected return that the provider of capital plans to earn on their investment.

Capital (money) used for funding a business should earn returns for the capital providers who risk their capital. For an investment to be worthwhile, the expected return on capital must be greater than the _____.

a. Cost of capital
c. BMC Software, Inc.
b. Capital flight
d. 3M Company

22. Discounting is a financial mechanism in which a debtor obtains the right to delay payments to a creditor, for a defined period of time, in exchange for a charge or fee. Essentially, the party that owes money in the present purchases the right to delay the payment until some future date. The _____, or charge, is simply the difference between the original amount owed in the present and the amount that has to be paid in the future to settle the debt.

a. Discount factor
c. Discounting
b. Risk aversion
d. Discount

23. The _____ is an interest rate a central bank charges depository institutions that borrow reserves from it.

The term _____ has two meanings:

- the same as interest rate; the term 'discount' does not refer to the meaning of the word, but to the purpose of using the quantity, such as computations of present value, e.g. net present value or discounted cash flow

- the annual effective _____, which is the annual interest divided by the capital including that interest; this rate is lower than the interest rate; it corresponds to using the value after a year as the nominal value, and seeing the initial value as the nominal value minus a discount; it is used for Treasury Bills and similar financial instruments

The annual effective _____ is the annual interest divided by the capital including that interest, which is the interest rate divided by 100% plus the interest rate. It is the annual discount factor to be applied to the future cash flow, to find the discount, subtracted from a future value to find the value one year earlier.

For example, suppose there is a government bond that sells for $95 and pays $100 in a year's time.

a. Discount rate
c. Convertible bond
b. Municipal bond
d. Process time

24. The _____ is a performance management tool which began as a concept for measuring whether the smaller-scale operational activities of a company are aligned with its larger-scale objectives in terms of vision and strategy.

By focusing not only on financial outcomes but also on the operational, marketing and developmental inputs to these, the _____ helps provide a more comprehensive view of a business, which in turn helps organizations act in their best long-term interests. This tool is also being used to address business response to climate change and greenhouse gas emissions.

a. Management by objectives
b. Best practice
c. Balanced Scorecard
d. Trustee

25. In economics, _____ is a rise in the general level of prices of goods and services in an economy over a period of time. When the general price level rises, each unit of currency buys fewer goods and services; consequently, _____ is also a decline in the real value of money--a loss of purchasing power in the medium of exchange which is also the monetary unit of account in the economy. A chief measure of general price-level _____ is the general _____ rate, which is the percentage change in a general price index (normally the Consumer Price Index) over time.
a. ABC Television Network
b. AIG
c. Opportunity cost
d. Inflation

26. The _____ is a private, not-for-profit organization whose primary purpose is to develop generally accepted accounting principles (GAAP) within the United States in the public's interest. The Securities and Exchange Commission (SEC) designated the _____ as the organization responsible for setting accounting standards for public companies in the U.S. It was created in 1973, replacing the Accounting Principles Board and the Committee on Accounting Procedure of the American Institute of Certified Public Accountants. The _____'s mission is 'to establish and improve standards of financial accounting and reporting for the guidance and education of the public, including issuers, auditors, and users of financial information.'

The _____ is not a governmental body.

a. Public company
b. Financial Accounting Standards Board
c. Governmental Accounting Standards Board
d. Fannie Mae

27. A _____ is a fungible, negotiable instrument representing financial value. they are broadly categorized into debt securities (such as banknotes, bonds and debentures), and equity securities; e.g., common stocks. The company or other entity issuing the _____ is called the issuer.
a. 3M Company
b. BMC Software, Inc.
c. Tracking stock
d. Security

28. The U.S. _____ is an independent agency of the United States government which holds primary responsibility for enforcing the federal securities laws and regulating the securities industry, the nation's stock and options exchanges, and other electronic securities markets. The SEC was created by section 4 of the Securities Exchange Act of 1934 (now codified as 15 U.S.C. ÂÂ§ 78d and commonly referred to as the 1934 Act.)
a. 3M Company
b. BNSF Railway
c. BMC Software, Inc.
d. Securities and Exchange Commission

29. In physics, and more specifically kinematics, _____ is the change in velocity over time. Because velocity is a vector, it can change in two ways: a change in magnitude and/or a change in direction. In one dimension, _____ is the rate at which something speeds up or slows down.
a. AIG
b. ABC Television Network
c. Acceleration
d. AMEX

30. The _____ is the current method of accelerated asset depreciation required by the United States income tax code. Under _____, all assets are divided into classes which dictate the number of years over which an asset's cost will be recovered.

Prior to the Accelerated Cost Recovery System (ACRS), most capital purchases were depreciated using a straight line technique, that allowed for the depreciation of the asset over its useful life.

a. BMC Software, Inc.
b. Categorical grants
c. Modified Accelerated Cost Recovery System
d. 3M Company

31. In business and accounting, _____ are everything of value that is owned by a person or company. It is a claim on the property your income of a borrower. The balance sheet of a firm records the monetary value of the _____ owned by the firm.

a. Assets
b. Accrual basis accounting
c. Accounts receivable
d. Earnings before interest, taxes, depreciation and amortization

32. In tax accounting the _____ is the default applicable convention used for federal income tax purposes. Like other conventions, the _____ affects the depreciation deduction computation in the year in which the property is placed into service. Using the _____, a taxpayer claims a half of a year's depreciation for the first taxable year, regardless of when the property was actually put into service.

a. Half-year convention
b. Reverse Morris trust
c. Taxable income
d. Revenue Procedures

33. _____ is any physical or virtual entity that is owned by an individual or jointly by a group of individuals. An owner of _____ has the right to consume, sell, rent, mortgage, transfer and exchange his or her _____. Important widely-recognized types of _____ include real _____, personal _____ (other physical possessions), and intellectual _____ (rights over artistic creations, inventions, etc.), although the latter is not always as widely recognized or enforced.

a. Disclosure requirement
b. Primary authority
c. Fiduciary
d. Property

34. _____ can be regarded as an outcome of mental processes (cognitive process) leading to the selection of a course of action among several alternatives. Every _____ process produces a final choice. The output can be an action or an opinion of choice.

a. BMC Software, Inc.
b. BNSF Railway
c. 3M Company
d. Decision making

35. Just in Time could refer to the following:

- _____, an inventory strategy that reduces in-process inventory
- _____ compilation, a technique for improving the performance of bytecode-compiled programming systems

a. Fiscal
b. Comparable
c. Help desk and incident reporting auditing
d. Just-in-time

36. A '_____' is the unit of an activity that causes the change of an activity cost. A _____ is any activity that causes a cost to be incurred. The Activity Based Costing (ABC) approach relates indirect cost to the activities that drive them to be incurred.

a. Cost driver
c. Factory overhead
b. Contribution margin analysis
d. Profit center

37. Straight-line depreciation is the simplest and most often used technique, in which the company estimates the _____ of the asset at the end of the period during which it will be used to generate revenues (useful life), and will expense a portion of original cost in equal increments over that period. The _____ is an estimate of the value of the asset at the time it will be sold or disposed of; it may be zero. _____ is scrap value, by another name.

a. Net profit
c. Closing entries
b. Generally accepted accounting principles
d. Salvage value

38. _____ is the study of how the variation (uncertainty) in the output of a mathematical model can be apportioned, qualitatively or quantitatively, to different sources of variation in the input of a model.

In more general terms uncertainty and sensitivity analyses investigate the robustness of a study when the study includes some form of mathematical modelling. While uncertainty analysis studies the overall uncertainty in the conclusions of the study, _____ tries to identify what source of uncertainty weights more on the study's conclusions.

a. Sensitivity analysis
c. Kaizen
b. Time to market
d. Free cash flow

39. _____ measures the nominal future sum of money that a given sum of money is 'worth' at a specified time in the future assuming a certain interest rate rate of return; it is the present value multiplied by the accumulation function.

The value does not include corrections for inflation or other factors that affect the true value of money in the future. This is used in time value of money calculations.

a. 3M Company
c. Present value
b. Net present value
d. Future value

40. The _____, P(T), is the number which a future cash flow, to be received at time T, must be multiplied by in order to obtain the current present value. Thus, a fixed annually compounded discount rate is

$$P(T) = \frac{1}{(1+r)^T}$$

For fixed continuously compounded discount rate we have

$$P(T) = e^{-rT}$$

For discounts in marketing, see discounts and allowances, sales promotion, and pricing.

a. Risk aversion
c. Risk
b. Risk adjusted return on capital
d. Discount factor

Chapter 13. Capital Investment Decisions

41. In mathematics _____s are numbers or other things that get multiplied. In particular, see:

- Factorization, the decomposition of an object into a product of other objects
- Integer factorization, the process of breaking down a composite number into smaller non-trivial divisors
- A coefficient
- A divisor of a particular number, or of an element of a monoid
- A von Neumann algebra with a trivial center

In statistics

- _____ analysis is the study of how _____s or certain variables affect variables.

In technology:

- Human _____s, a profession that focuses on how people interact with products, tools, or procedures
- 'Functionality, Application domain, Conditions, Technology, Objects and Responsibility;', In object-oriented programming

In computer science and information technology:

- Authentication _____, a piece of information used to verify a person's identity for security purposes
- _____, a Unix command for numbers factorization
- _____ (programming language), an experimental Forth-like programming language

In television:

- The O'Reilly _____, an American talk show hosted by Bill O'Reilly on Fox News.
- The Krypton _____, a British game show hosted by Gordon Burns, formally on ITV. Also had an American version.

a. Merck ' Co., Inc.
b. Valuation
c. The Goodyear Tire ' Rubber Company
d. Factor

42. _____ is a fee paid on borrowed assets. It is the price paid for the use of borrowed money, or, money earned by deposited funds .Assets that are sometimes lent with _____ include money, shares, consumer goods through hire purchase, major assets such as aircraft, and even entire factories in finance lease arrangements. The _____ is calculated upon the value of the assets in the same manner as upon money.

a. ABC Television Network
b. Interest
c. Insolvency
d. AIG

43. The term _____ is used in finance theory to refer to any terminating stream of fixed payments over a specified period of time. This usage is most commonly seen in academic discussions of finance, usually in connection with the valuation of the stream of payments, taking into account time value of money concepts such as interest rate and future value.

Examples of these are regular deposits to a savings account, monthly home mortgage payments and monthly insurance payments.

a. Intangible
c. Appropriation

b. Improvement
d. Annuity

Chapter 14. Inventory Management

1. An _____ is a term used in behavioral economics to describe those types of behaviors that impose costs on a person in the long-run that are not taken into account when making decisions in the present. Classical Economics discourages government from creating legislation that targets internalities, because it is assumed that the consumer takes these personal costs into account when paying for the good that causes the _____. For example, cigarettes should be taxed because of the negative consumption externalities that they impose, such as second-hand smoke, not because the smoker harms him or herself by smoking.

   a. Inventory turnover ratio
   b. Authorised capital
   c. Operating budget
   d. Internality

2. The _____ is the United States federal government agency that collects taxes and enforces the internal revenue laws. It is an agency within the U.S. Dept of the treasury responsible for interpretation and application of Federal tax law. The official U.S. Treasury regulations provide (in part):

   The _____ is a bureau of the Department of the Treasury under the immediate direction of the Commissioner of Internal Revenue.

   a. Indirect tax
   b. Use tax
   c. Income tax
   d. Internal Revenue Service

3. An _____ is a practitioner of accountancy, which is the measurement, disclosure or provision of assurance about financial information that helps managers, investors, tax authorities and other decision makers make resource allocation decisions.

   The word '_____' is derived from the French 'Compter' which took its origin from the Latin 'Computare'. The word was formerly written in English as 'Accomptant', but in process of time the word, which was always pronounced by dropping the 'p', became gradually changed both in pronunciation and in orthography to its present form.

   a. Accountant
   b. AIG
   c. ABC Television Network
   d. AMEX

4. The _____ is a professional organization headquartered in Montvale, New Jersey consisting of over 70,000 members worldwide. The IMA is dedicated to advancing the role of the management accountant and financial manager within the business organization, and provides relevant professional certification.

   The IMA awards the Certified Management Accountant (CMA) designation in the United States.

   a. International Accounting Standards Committee
   b. Institute of Management Accountants
   c. American Accounting Association
   d. Emerging technologies

5. _____ is concerned with the provisions and use of accounting information to managers within organizations, to provide them with the basis to make informed business decisions that will allow them to be better equipped in their management and control functions.

Chapter 14. Inventory Management

In contrast to financial accountancy information, _____ information is:

- usually confidential and used by management, instead of publicly reported;
- forward-looking, instead of historical;
- pragmatically computed using extensive management information systems and internal controls, instead of complying with accounting standards.

This is because of the different emphasis: _____ information is used within an organization, typically for decision-making.

a. Management accounting
b. Nonassurance services
c. Governmental accounting
d. Grenzplankostenrechnung

6. A _____ is a fungible, negotiable instrument representing financial value. they are broadly categorized into debt securities (such as banknotes, bonds and debentures), and equity securities; e.g., common stocks. The company or other entity issuing the _____ is called the issuer.

a. Tracking stock
b. 3M Company
c. BMC Software, Inc.
d. Security

7. The U.S. _____ is an independent agency of the United States government which holds primary responsibility for enforcing the federal securities laws and regulating the securities industry, the nation's stock and options exchanges, and other electronic securities markets. The SEC was created by section 4 of the Securities Exchange Act of 1934 (now codified as 15 U.S.C. ÂÂ§ 78d and commonly referred to as the 1934 Act.)

a. Securities and Exchange Commission
b. BNSF Railway
c. 3M Company
d. BMC Software, Inc.

8. In economics, business, retail, and accounting, a _____ is the value of money that has been used up to produce something, and hence is not available for use anymore. In economics, a _____ is an alternative that is given up as a result of a decision. In business, the _____ may be one of acquisition, in which case the amount of money expended to acquire it is counted as _____.

a. Prime cost
b. Cost allocation
c. Cost
d. Cost of quality

9. _____ is the process whereby companies use cost accounting to report or control the various costs of doing business.

The term _____ is widely used in business today. Unfortunately _____ has no uniform definition.

a. Contribution margin analysis
b. Contribution margin
c. Cost management
d. Process costing

10. A _____ is the period of time between the initiation of any process of production and the completion of that process. Thus the _____ for ordering a new car from a manufacturer may be anywhere from 2 weeks to 6 months. In industry, _____ reduction is an important part of lean manufacturing.

Chapter 14. Inventory Management

a. 3M Company
c. BNSF Railway
b. BMC Software, Inc.
d. Lead time

11. The _____ is the level of inventory when a fresh order should be made with suppliers to bring the inventory up by the Economic order quantity ('EOQ'.)

The _____ for replenishment of stock occurs when the level of inventory drops down to zero. In view of instantaneous replenishment of stock the level of inventory jumps to the original level from zero level.

a. FIFO and LIFO accounting
c. 3M Company
b. Reorder point
d. Finished good

12. _____ is a term used by inventory specialists to describe a level of extra stock that is maintained below the cycle stock to buffer against stockouts. _____ exists to counter uncertainties in supply and demand. _____ is defined as extra units of inventory carried as protection against possible stockouts .(shortfall in raw material or packaging.)

a. Proprietorship
c. Tax profit
b. Sensitivity analysis
d. Safety stock

13. _____ refers to a business or organization attempting to acquire goods or services to accomplish the goals of the enterprise. Though there are several organizations that attempt to set standards in the _____ process, processes can vary greatly between organizations. Typically the word e;_____e; is not used interchangeably with the word e;procuremente;, since procurement typically includes Expediting, Supplier Quality, and Traffic and Logistics (T'L) in addition to _____.

a. Purchasing
c. Supply chain
b. Free port
d. Consignor

14. Just in Time could refer to the following:

- _____, an inventory strategy that reduces in-process inventory
- _____ compilation, a technique for improving the performance of bytecode-compiled programming systems

a. Help desk and incident reporting auditing
c. Fiscal
b. Comparable
d. Just-in-time

15. _____ is one of the four Ps of the marketing mix. The other three aspects are product, promotion, and place. It is also a key variable in microeconomic price allocation theory.

a. Cost-plus pricing
c. Pricing
b. Price
d. Target costing

16. _____ refers to the pricing of contributions (assets, tangible and intangible, services, and funds) transferred within an organization. For example, goods from the production division may be sold to the marketing division, or goods from a parent company may be sold to a foreign subsidiary. Since the prices are set within an organization (i.e. controlled), the typical market mechanisms that establish prices for such transactions between third parties may not apply.

a. Price
b. Transactional Net Margin Method
c. Pricing
d. Transfer pricing

17. The _____ is a performance management tool which began as a concept for measuring whether the smaller-scale operational activities of a company are aligned with its larger-scale objectives in terms of vision and strategy.

By focusing not only on financial outcomes but also on the operational, marketing and developmental inputs to these, the _____ helps provide a more comprehensive view of a business, which in turn helps organizations act in their best long-term interests. This tool is also being used to address business response to climate change and greenhouse gas emissions.

a. Management by objectives
b. Best practice
c. Trustee
d. Balanced Scorecard

18. _____ is an accounting methodology that traces and accumulates direct costs, and allocates indirect costs of a manufacturing process. Costs are assigned to products, usually in a large batch, which might include an entire month's production. Eventually, costs have to be allocated to individual units of product.

a. Profit center
b. Cost driver
c. Cost management
d. Process costing

19. In business, _____, Overhead cost or _____ expense refers to an ongoing expense of operating a business. The term _____ is usually used to group expenses that are necessary to the continued functioning of the business, but do not directly generate profits.

_____ expenses are all costs on the income statement except for direct labor and direct materials.

a. Intangible assets
b. ABC Television Network
c. AIG
d. Overhead

20. In engineering and manufacturing, _____ and quality engineering are used in developing systems to ensure products or services are designed and produced to meet or exceed customer requirements. Refer to the definition by Merriam-Webster for further information. These systems are often developed in conjunction with other business and engineering disciplines using a cross-functional approach.

a. BNSF Railway
b. 3M Company
c. Quality control
d. BMC Software, Inc.

21. In financial accounting, a _____ is defined as an obligation of an entity arising from past transactions or events, the settlement of which may result in the transfer or use of assets, provision of services or other yielding of economic benefits in the future.

a. Liability
b. False Claims Act
c. Corporate governance
d. Vested

22. _____ refers to the structured transmission of data between organizations by electronic means. It is used to transfer electronic documents from one computer system to another (ie) from one trading partner to another trading partner. It is more than mere E-mail; for instance, organizations might replace bills of lading and even checks with appropriate _____ messages.

a. AIG
b. Electronic data interchange
c. Electronic commerce
d. ABC Television Network

23. _____ is an acronym for First In, First Out, an abstraction in ways of organizing and manipulation of data relative to time and prioritization. This expression describes the principle of a queue processing technique or servicing conflicting demands by ordering process by first-come, first-served (FCFS) behaviour: what comes in first is handled first, what comes in next waits until the first is finished, etc.

Thus it is analogous to the behaviour of persons queueing (or 'standing in line', in common American parlance), where the persons leave the queue in the order they arrive, or waiting one's turn at a traffic control signal.

a. Trademark
b. Risk management
c. Kanban
d. FIFO

24. _____ is a concept related to lean and just-in-time (JIT) production. The Japanese word _____ is a common everyday term meaning 'signboard' or 'billboard' and utterly lacks the specialized meaning that this loanword has acquired in English. According to Taiichi Ohno, the man credited with developing JIT, _____ is a means through which JIT is achieved.

a. Trademark
b. Kanban
c. FIFO
d. Risk management

25. Discounting is a financial mechanism in which a debtor obtains the right to delay payments to a creditor, for a defined period of time, in exchange for a charge or fee. Essentially, the party that owes money in the present purchases the right to delay the payment until some future date. The _____, or charge, is simply the difference between the original amount owed in the present and the amount that has to be paid in the future to settle the debt.

a. Discount factor
b. Risk aversion
c. Discounting
d. Discount

26. _____ in economics and business is the result of an exchange and from that trade we assign a numerical monetary value to a good, service or asset. If Alice trades Bob 4 apples for an orange, the _____ of an orange is 4 apples. Inversely, the _____ of an apple is 1/4 oranges.

a. Price
b. Discounts and allowances
c. Transactional Net Margin Method
d. Price discrimination

27. In accounting, _____ has a very specific meaning. It is an outflow of cash or other valuable assets from a person or company to another person or company. This outflow of cash is generally one side of a trade for products or services that have equal or better current or future value to the buyer than to the seller.

a. AIG
b. AMEX
c. ABC Television Network
d. Expense

28. An _____, operating expenditure, operational expense, operational expenditure or OPEX is an on-going cost for running a product, business, or system. Its counterpart, a capital expenditure (CAPEX), is the cost of developing or providing non-consumable parts for the product or system. For example, the purchase of a photocopier is the CAPEX, and the annual paper and toner cost is the OPEX.

a. AMEX
b. AIG
c. ABC Television Network
d. Operating expense

29. _____ is an overall management philosophy introduced by Dr. Eliyahu M. Goldratt in his 1984 book titled The Goal, that is geared to help organizations continually achieve their goal. The title comes from the contention that any manageable system is limited in achieving more of its goal by a very small number of constraints, and that there is always at least one constraint. The _____ process seeks to identify the constraint and restructure the rest of the organization around it, through the use of the Five Focusing Steps.
   a. Six Sigma
   b. Lean production
   c. Lean manufacturing
   d. Theory of constraints

30. The concept of quality costs is a means to quantify the total _____-related efforts and deficiencies. It was first described by Armand V. Feigenbaum in a 1956 Harvard Business Review article.

Prior to its introduction, the general perception was that higher quality requires higher costs, either by buying better materials or machines or by hiring more labor.

   a. Cost accounting
   b. Quality costs
   c. Marginal cost
   d. Cost of quality

31. A _____ is an entity formed between two or more parties to undertake economic activity together. The parties agree to create a new entity by both contributing equity, and they then share in the revenues, expenses, and control of the enterprise. The venture can be for one specific project only, or a continuing business relationship such as the Fuji Xerox _____.
   a. Fraud Enforcement and Recovery Act
   b. Chief Financial Officers Act of 1990
   c. Pre-emption right
   d. Joint venture

Chapter 15. Quality Costs and Productivity: Measurement, Reporting, and Control

1. In economics, business, retail, and accounting, a _____ is the value of money that has been used up to produce something, and hence is not available for use anymore. In economics, a _____ is an alternative that is given up as a result of a decision. In business, the _____ may be one of acquisition, in which case the amount of money expended to acquire it is counted as _____.
   a. Prime cost
   b. Cost
   c. Cost allocation
   d. Cost of quality

2. _____ in economics refers to metrics and measures of output from production processes, per unit of input. Labor _____, for example, is typically measured as a ratio of output per labor-hour, an input. _____ may be conceived of as a metrics of the technical or engineering efficiency of production.
   a. Cellular manufacturing
   b. Deming Prize
   c. Value engineering
   d. Productivity

3. The concept of _____ is a means to quantify the total cost of quality-related efforts and deficiencies. It was first described by Armand V. Feigenbaum in a 1956 Harvard Business Review article.

   Prior to its introduction, the general perception was that higher quality requires higher costs, either by buying better materials or machines or by hiring more labor.

   a. Marginal cost
   b. Quality costs
   c. Cost allocation
   d. Variable cost

4. The _____ is a private, not-for-profit organization whose primary purpose is to develop generally accepted accounting principles (GAAP) within the United States in the public's interest. The Securities and Exchange Commission (SEC) designated the _____ as the organization responsible for setting accounting standards for public companies in the U.S. It was created in 1973, replacing the Accounting Principles Board and the Committee on Accounting Procedure of the American Institute of Certified Public Accountants. The _____'s mission is 'to establish and improve standards of financial accounting and reporting for the guidance and education of the public, including issuers, auditors, and users of financial information.'

   The _____ is not a governmental body.

   a. Financial Accounting Standards Board
   b. Governmental Accounting Standards Board
   c. Public company
   d. Fannie Mae

5. A _____ is an entity formed between two or more parties to undertake economic activity together. The parties agree to create a new entity by both contributing equity, and they then share in the revenues, expenses, and control of the enterprise. The venture can be for one specific project only, or a continuing business relationship such as the Fuji Xerox _____.
   a. Joint venture
   b. Fraud Enforcement and Recovery Act
   c. Chief Financial Officers Act of 1990
   d. Pre-emption right

6. The term '_____' refers to the concept of collecting information and attempting to spot a pattern in the information. In some fields of study, the term '_____' has more formally-defined meanings.

   In project management _____ is a mathematical technique that uses historical results to predict future outcome.

Chapter 15. Quality Costs and Productivity: Measurement, Reporting, and Control

a. 3M Company
c. Multicollinearity
b. Regression analysis
d. Trend analysis

7. In financial accounting, a _____ is defined as an obligation of an entity arising from past transactions or events, the settlement of which may result in the transfer or use of assets, provision of services or other yielding of economic benefits in the future.

a. Corporate governance
c. Liability
b. Vested
d. False Claims Act

8. '_____' is Step 7 of 'Philip Crosby's 14 Step Quality Improvement Process' . Although applicable to any type of enterprise, it has been primarily adopted within industry supply chains wherever large volumes of components are being purchased (common items such as nuts and bolts are good examples.)

_____ was a quality control program originated by the Denver Division of the Martin Marietta Corporation (now Lockheed Martin) on the Titan Missile program, which carried the first astronauts into space in the late 1960s.

a. 3M Company
c. BNSF Railway
b. Zero defects
d. BMC Software, Inc.

9. The _____ is a performance management tool which began as a concept for measuring whether the smaller-scale operational activities of a company are aligned with its larger-scale objectives in terms of vision and strategy.

By focusing not only on financial outcomes but also on the operational, marketing and developmental inputs to these, the _____ helps provide a more comprehensive view of a business, which in turn helps organizations act in their best long-term interests. This tool is also being used to address business response to climate change and greenhouse gas emissions.

a. Management by objectives
c. Balanced Scorecard
b. Best practice
d. Trustee

10. _____ is concerned with the provisions and use of accounting information to managers within organizations, to provide them with the basis to make informed business decisions that will allow them to be better equipped in their management and control functions.

In contrast to financial accountancy information, _____ information is:

- usually confidential and used by management, instead of publicly reported;
- forward-looking, instead of historical;
- pragmatically computed using extensive management information systems and internal controls, instead of complying with accounting standards.

This is because of the different emphasis: _____ information is used within an organization, typically for decision-making.

a. Management Accounting
c. Grenzplankostenrechnung
b. Governmental accounting
d. Nonassurance services

11. A _____ is any one of a variety of different systems, institutions, procedures, social relations and infrastructures whereby persons trade, and goods and services are exchanged, forming part of the economy. It is an arrangement that allows buyers and sellers to exchange things. _____s vary in size, range, geographic scale, location, types and variety of human communities, as well as the types of goods and services traded.

a. Market
c. Perfect competition
b. Market Failure
d. Recession

12. In engineering and manufacturing, _____ and quality engineering are used in developing systems to ensure products or services are designed and produced to meet or exceed customer requirements. Refer to the definition by Merriam-Webster for further information. These systems are often developed in conjunction with other business and engineering disciplines using a cross-functional approach.

a. BNSF Railway
c. 3M Company
b. BMC Software, Inc.
d. Quality control

13. _____ is the process whereby companies use cost accounting to report or control the various costs of doing business.

The term _____ is widely used in business today. Unfortunately _____ has no uniform definition.

a. Cost management
c. Process costing
b. Contribution margin
d. Contribution margin analysis

14. American Society for Quality (ASQ), formerly known as _____, is a knowledge-based global community of quality control experts, with nearly 85,000 members dedicated to the promotion and advancement of quality tools, principles, and practices in their workplaces and in their communities.

Established in 1946 and based in Milwaukee, ASQ traces its beginnings to the end of World War II, as quality experts and manufacturers sought ways to sustain the many quality-improvement techniques used during wartime. ASQ has played an important role in upholding these standards from the past while championing continued innovation in the field of quality.

a. AIG
c. ABC Television Network
b. International Monetary Fund
d. American Society for Quality Control

15. An _____ is a practitioner of accountancy, which is the measurement, disclosure or provision of assurance about financial information that helps managers, investors, tax authorities and other decision makers make resource allocation decisions.

The word '_____' is derived from the French 'Compter' which took its origin from the Latin 'Computare'. The word was formerly written in English as 'Accomptant', but in process of time the word, which was always pronounced by dropping the 'p', became gradually changed both in pronunciation and in orthography to its present form.

Chapter 15. Quality Costs and Productivity: Measurement, Reporting, and Control

a. AMEX
c. AIG
b. ABC Television Network
d. Accountant

16. The _____ is a professional organization headquartered in Montvale, New Jersey consisting of over 70,000 members worldwide. The IMA is dedicated to advancing the role of the management accountant and financial manager within the business organization, and provides relevant professional certification.

The IMA awards the Certified Management Accountant (CMA) designation in the United States.

a. American Accounting Association
c. International Accounting Standards Committee
b. Institute of Management Accountants
d. Emerging technologies

17. _____ is one of the four Ps of the marketing mix. The other three aspects are product, promotion, and place. It is also a key variable in microeconomic price allocation theory.

a. Price
c. Cost-plus pricing
b. Target costing
d. Pricing

18. _____ is an acronym for First In, First Out, an abstraction in ways of organizing and manipulation of data relative to time and prioritization. This expression describes the principle of a queue processing technique or servicing conflicting demands by ordering process by first-come, first-served (FCFS) behaviour: what comes in first is handled first, what comes in next waits until the first is finished, etc.

Thus it is analogous to the behaviour of persons queueing (or 'standing in line', in common American parlance), where the persons leave the queue in the order they arrive, or waiting one's turn at a traffic control signal.

a. Kanban
c. FIFO
b. Risk management
d. Trademark

19. _____ is a demonstration of a process -- such as a variable, term, or object -- relative in terms of the specific process or set of validation tests used to determine its presence and quantity. Properties described in this manner must be sufficiently accessible, so that persons other than the definer may independently measure or test for them at will. An _____ is generally designed to model a conceptual definition.

a. AIG
c. AMEX
b. ABC Television Network
d. Operational definition

20. _____ is a model for workplace design, and is an integral part of lean manufacturing systems. The goal of lean manufacturing is the aggressive minimisation of waste, called muda, to achieve maximum efficiency of resources. _____, sometimes called cellular or cell production, arranges factory floor labor into semi-autonomous and multi-skilled teams, or work cells, who manufacture complete products or complex components.

a. Value engineering
c. Changeover
b. Cellular manufacturing
d. Productivity

Chapter 16. Lean Accounting, Target Costing, and the Balanced Scorecard

1. _____ is accounting for the lean enterprise. It seeks to move from traditional cost accounting to a system that measures and motivates good business practices in the lean enterprise.

Lean manufacturing methods were first introduced into the United States and other Western countries in the 1980's; primarily by the Toyota companies.

   a. BNSF Railway
   b. 3M Company
   c. Lean accounting
   d. BMC Software, Inc.

2. _____ or lean production, which is often known simply as 'Lean', is a production practice that considers the expenditure of resources for any goal other than the creation of value for the end customer to be wasteful, and thus a target for elimination. Working from the perspective of the customer who consumes a product or service, 'value' is defined as any action or process that a customer would be willing to pay for. Basically, lean is centered around creating more value with less work.

   a. Lean production
   b. Lean manufacturing
   c. Theory of constraints
   d. Six Sigma

3. _____ is an acronym for First In, First Out, an abstraction in ways of organizing and manipulation of data relative to time and prioritization. This expression describes the principle of a queue processing technique or servicing conflicting demands by ordering process by first-come, first-served (FCFS) behaviour: what comes in first is handled first, what comes in next waits until the first is finished, etc.

Thus it is analogous to the behaviour of persons queueing (or 'standing in line', in common American parlance), where the persons leave the queue in the order they arrive, or waiting one's turn at a traffic control signal.

   a. Kanban
   b. FIFO
   c. Trademark
   d. Risk management

4. A _____ is an entity formed between two or more parties to undertake economic activity together. The parties agree to create a new entity by both contributing equity, and they then share in the revenues, expenses, and control of the enterprise. The venture can be for one specific project only, or a continuing business relationship such as the Fuji Xerox _____.

   a. Chief Financial Officers Act of 1990
   b. Fraud Enforcement and Recovery Act
   c. Pre-emption right
   d. Joint venture

5. Just in Time could refer to the following:

   - _____, an inventory strategy that reduces in-process inventory
   - _____ compilation, a technique for improving the performance of bytecode-compiled programming systems

   a. Comparable
   b. Fiscal
   c. Just-in-time
   d. Help desk and incident reporting auditing

Chapter 16. Lean Accounting, Target Costing, and the Balanced Scorecard

6. _____ refers to a business or organization attempting to acquire goods or services to accomplish the goals of the enterprise. Though there are several organizations that attempt to set standards in the _____ process, processes can vary greatly between organizations. Typically the word e;_____e; is not used interchangeably with the word e;procuremente;, since procurement typically includes Expediting, Supplier Quality, and Traffic and Logistics (T'L) in addition to _____.
   a. Purchasing
   b. Consignor
   c. Supply chain
   d. Free port

7. _____ is concerned with the provisions and use of accounting information to managers within organizations, to provide them with the basis to make informed business decisions that will allow them to be better equipped in their management and control functions.

In contrast to financial accountancy information, _____ information is:

- usually confidential and used by management, instead of publicly reported;
- forward-looking, instead of historical;
- pragmatically computed using extensive management information systems and internal controls, instead of complying with accounting standards.

This is because of the different emphasis: _____ information is used within an organization, typically for decision-making.

   a. Nonassurance services
   b. Governmental accounting
   c. Management Accounting
   d. Grenzplankostenrechnung

8. _____ is an accounting methodology that traces and accumulates direct costs, and allocates indirect costs of a manufacturing process. Costs are assigned to products, usually in a large batch, which might include an entire month's production. Eventually, costs have to be allocated to individual units of product.
   a. Cost management
   b. Profit center
   c. Cost driver
   d. Process costing

9. The _____ is a performance management tool which began as a concept for measuring whether the smaller-scale operational activities of a company are aligned with its larger-scale objectives in terms of vision and strategy.

By focusing not only on financial outcomes but also on the operational, marketing and developmental inputs to these, the _____ helps provide a more comprehensive view of a business, which in turn helps organizations act in their best long-term interests. This tool is also being used to address business response to climate change and greenhouse gas emissions.

   a. Trustee
   b. Management by objectives
   c. Best practice
   d. Balanced Scorecard

Chapter 16. Lean Accounting, Target Costing, and the Balanced Scorecard

10. _____ is the acquisition of goods and/or services at the best possible total cost of ownership, in the right quantity and quality, at the right time, in the right place and from the right source for the direct benefit or use of corporations or individuals, generally via a contract. Simple _____ may involve nothing more than repeat purchasing. Complex _____ could involve finding long term partners - or even 'co-destiny' suppliers that might fundamentally commit one organization to another.
   a. Customer satisfaction
   b. Free cash flow
   c. Time to market
   d. Procurement

11. In engineering and manufacturing, _____ and quality engineering are used in developing systems to ensure products or services are designed and produced to meet or exceed customer requirements. Refer to the definition by Merriam-Webster for further information . These systems are often developed in conjunction with other business and engineering disciplines using a cross-functional approach.
   a. BNSF Railway
   b. BMC Software, Inc.
   c. 3M Company
   d. Quality control

12. _____ is a method of identifying and evaluating activities that a business performs using activity-based costing to carry out a value chain analysis or a re-engineering initiative to improve strategic and operational decisions in an organization. Activity-based costing establishes relationships between overhead costs and activities so that overhead costs can be more precisely allocated to products, services, or customer segments. _____ focuses on managing activities to reduce costs and improve customer value.
   a. ABC Television Network
   b. Indirect costs
   c. Activity-based costing
   d. Activity-based management

13. In economics, business, retail, and accounting, a _____ is the value of money that has been used up to produce something, and hence is not available for use anymore. In economics, a _____ is an alternative that is given up as a result of a decision. In business, the _____ may be one of acquisition, in which case the amount of money expended to acquire it is counted as _____.
   a. Cost
   b. Prime cost
   c. Cost of quality
   d. Cost allocation

14. In business, _____, Overhead cost or _____ expense refers to an ongoing expense of operating a business. The term _____ is usually used to group expenses that are necessary to the continued functioning of the business, but do not directly generate profits.

   _____ expenses are all costs on the income statement except for direct labor and direct materials.

   a. Overhead
   b. AIG
   c. Intangible assets
   d. ABC Television Network

15. An _____ is a practitioner of accountancy, which is the measurement, disclosure or provision of assurance about financial information that helps managers, investors, tax authorities and other decision makers make resource allocation decisions.

Chapter 16. Lean Accounting, Target Costing, and the Balanced Scorecard 91

The word '_____' is derived from the French 'Compter' which took its origin from the Latin 'Computare'. The word was formerly written in English as 'Accomptant', but in process of time the word, which was always pronounced by dropping the 'p', became gradually changed both in pronunciation and in orthography to its present form.

a. ABC Television Network
c. AIG

b. AMEX
d. Accountant

16. The _____ is a professional organization headquartered in Montvale, New Jersey consisting of over 70,000 members worldwide. The IMA is dedicated to advancing the role of the management accountant and financial manager within the business organization, and provides relevant professional certification.

The IMA awards the Certified Management Accountant (CMA) designation in the United States.

a. Emerging technologies
c. International Accounting Standards Committee

b. American Accounting Association
d. Institute of Management Accountants

17. An _____ is a term used in behavioral economics to describe those types of behaviors that impose costs on a person in the long-run that are not taken into account when making decisions in the present. Classical Economics discourages government from creating legislation that targets internalities, because it is assumed that the consumer takes these personal costs into account when paying for the good that causes the _____. For example, cigarettes should be taxed because of the negative consumption externalities that they impose, such as second-hand smoke, not because the smoker harms him or herself by smoking.

a. Authorised capital
c. Inventory turnover ratio

b. Internality
d. Operating budget

18. _____ can be regarded as an outcome of mental processes (cognitive process) leading to the selection of a course of action among several alternatives. Every _____ process produces a final choice. The output can be an action or an opinion of choice.

a. 3M Company
c. BNSF Railway

b. Decision making
d. BMC Software, Inc.

19. _____ describes the situation when output from (or information about the result of) an event or phenomenon in the past will influence the same event/phenomenon in the present or future. When an event is part of a chain of cause-and-effect that forms a circuit or loop, then the event is said to 'feed back' into itself.

_____ is also a synonym for:

- _____ Signal; the information about the initial event that is the basis for subsequent modification of the event.
- _____ Loop; the causal path that leads from the initial generation of the _____ signal to the subsequent modification of the event.

_____ is a mechanism, process or signal that is looped back to control a system within itself. Such a loop is called a _____ loop.

a. 3M Company
c. Controllable

b. Feedback
d. BMC Software, Inc.

20. _____ is the process whereby an organization establishes the parameters within which programs, investments, and acquisitions are reaching the desired results. Performance Reference Model of the Federal Enterprise Architecture, 2005.

This process of measuring performance often requires the use of statistical evidence to determine progress toward specific defined organizational objectives.

There are many types of measurements.

a. Management by exception
c. Management by objectives

b. Performance measurement
d. Trustee

21. _____ is the process whereby companies use cost accounting to report or control the various costs of doing business.

The term _____ is widely used in business today. Unfortunately _____ has no uniform definition.

a. Contribution margin
c. Process costing

b. Contribution margin analysis
d. Cost management

22. _____ is a pricing method used by firms. It is defined as 'a cost management tool for reducing the overall cost of a product over its entire life-cycle with the help of production, engineering, research and design'. A target cost is the maximum amount of cost that can be incurred on a product and with it the firm can still earn the required profit margin from that product at a particular selling price.

a. Penetration pricing
c. Discounts and allowances

b. Pricing
d. Target costing

23. The _____ is a concept from business management that was first described and popularized by Michael Porter in his 1985 best-seller, Competitive Advantage: Creating and Sustaining Superior Performance.

A _____ is a chain of activities. Products pass through all activities of the chain in order and at each activity the product gains some value.

a. Value chain
c. Product differentiation

b. Customer relationship management
d. Market segmentation

24. The _____ is a private, not-for-profit organization whose primary purpose is to develop generally accepted accounting principles (GAAP) within the United States in the public's interest. The Securities and Exchange Commission (SEC) designated the _____ as the organization responsible for setting accounting standards for public companies in the U.S. It was created in 1973, replacing the Accounting Principles Board and the Committee on Accounting Procedure of the American Institute of Certified Public Accountants. The _____'s mission is 'to establish and improve standards of financial accounting and reporting for the guidance and education of the public, including issuers, auditors, and users of financial information.'

Chapter 16. Lean Accounting, Target Costing, and the Balanced Scorecard

The _____ is not a governmental body.

a. Governmental Accounting Standards Board
b. Public company
c. Financial Accounting Standards Board
d. Fannie Mae

25. A _____, also client, buyer or purchaser is the buyer or user of the paid products of an individual or organization, mostly called the supplier or seller. This is typically through purchasing or renting goods or services.
   a. BNSF Railway
   b. 3M Company
   c. Customer
   d. BMC Software, Inc.

26. In financial accounting, a _____ is defined as an obligation of an entity arising from past transactions or events, the settlement of which may result in the transfer or use of assets, provision of services or other yielding of economic benefits in the future.
   a. Liability
   b. Corporate governance
   c. Vested
   d. False Claims Act

27. In physics, _____ is defined as the rate of change of position. It is a vector physical quantity; both speed and direction are required to define it. In the SI (metric) system, it is measured in meters per second: (m/s) or ms^{-1}.
   a. Velocity
   b. NASDAQ
   c. Job fraud
   d. P/E ratio

28. In finance, the term _____ describes the amount in cash that returns to the owners of a security. Normally it does not include the price variations, at the difference of the total return. _____ applies to various stated rates of return on stocks (common and preferred, and convertible), fixed income instruments (bonds, notes, bills, strips, zero coupon), and some other investment type insurance products (e.g. annuities.)
   a. Residence trusts
   b. Pension System
   c. Disclosure
   d. Yield

29. Employment is a contract between two parties, one being the employer and the other being the _____. An _____ may be defined as: 'A person in the service of another under any contract of hire, express or implied, oral or written, where the employer has the power or right to control and direct the _____ in the material details of how the work is to be performed.' Black's Law Dictionary page 471 (5th ed. 1979.)
   a. Employee
   b. AMEX
   c. ABC Television Network
   d. AIG

30. _____ refers to increasing the spiritual, political, social or economic strength of individuals and communities. It often involves the empowered developing confidence in their own capacities.

The term Human _____ covers a vast landscape of meanings, interpretations, definitions and disciplines ranging from psychology and philosophy to the highly commercialized Self-Help industry and Motivational sciences.

a. IMF
b. IPO
c. Entity
d. Empowerment

31. The _____ is a United States law enacted in 1993. It is one of a series of laws designed to improve government project management. The GPRA requires agencies to engage in project management tasks such as setting goals, measuring results, and reporting their progress.

a. BNSF Railway
b. BMC Software, Inc.
c. 3M Company
d. Government Performance and Results Act

Chapter 17. Environmental Cost Management

1. In economics, business, retail, and accounting, a _____ is the value of money that has been used up to produce something, and hence is not available for use anymore. In economics, a _____ is an alternative that is given up as a result of a decision. In business, the _____ may be one of acquisition, in which case the amount of money expended to acquire it is counted as _____.

   a. Prime cost
   b. Cost of quality
   c. Cost allocation
   d. Cost

2. _____ is the process whereby companies use cost accounting to report or control the various costs of doing business.

   The term _____ is widely used in business today. Unfortunately _____ has no uniform definition.

   a. Contribution margin analysis
   b. Contribution margin
   c. Process costing
   d. Cost management

3. An _____ is a practitioner of accountancy, which is the measurement, disclosure or provision of assurance about financial information that helps managers, investors, tax authorities and other decision makers make resource allocation decisions.

   The word '_____' is derived from the French 'Compter' which took its origin from the Latin 'Computare'. The word was formerly written in English as 'Accomptant', but in process of time the word, which was always pronounced by dropping the 'p', became gradually changed both in pronunciation and in orthography to its present form.

   a. AMEX
   b. ABC Television Network
   c. AIG
   d. Accountant

4. The _____ is a professional organization headquartered in Montvale, New Jersey consisting of over 70,000 members worldwide. The IMA is dedicated to advancing the role of the management accountant and financial manager within the business organization, and provides relevant professional certification.

   The IMA awards the Certified Management Accountant (CMA) designation in the United States.

   a. American Accounting Association
   b. Emerging technologies
   c. International Accounting Standards Committee
   d. Institute of Management Accountants

5. _____ is concerned with the provisions and use of accounting information to managers within organizations, to provide them with the basis to make informed business decisions that will allow them to be better equipped in their management and control functions.

   In contrast to financial accountancy information, _____ information is:

   - usually confidential and used by management, instead of publicly reported;
   - forward-looking, instead of historical;
   - pragmatically computed using extensive management information systems and internal controls, instead of complying with accounting standards.

Chapter 17. Environmental Cost Management

This is because of the different emphasis: _____ information is used within an organization, typically for decision-making.

a. Management accounting
c. Grenzplankostenrechnung
b. Governmental accounting
d. Nonassurance services

6. _____ is a pattern of resource use that aims to meet human needs while preserving the environment so that these needs can be met not only in the present, but also for future generations to come. The term was used by the Brundtland Commission which coined what has become the most often-quoted definition of _____ as development that 'meets the needs of the present without compromising the ability of future generations to meet their own needs.'

_____ ties together concern for the carrying capacity of natural systems with the social challenges facing humanity. As early as the 1970s 'sustainability' was employed to describe an economy 'in equilibrium with basic ecological support systems.' Ecologists have pointed to the e;limits of growthe; and presented the alternative of a e;steady state economye; in order to address environmental concerns.

a. Time value of money
c. Limited liability company
b. Collusion
d. Sustainable development

7. _____ is an acronym for First In, First Out, an abstraction in ways of organizing and manipulation of data relative to time and prioritization. This expression describes the principle of a queue processing technique or servicing conflicting demands by ordering process by first-come, first-served (FCFS) behaviour: what comes in first is handled first, what comes in next waits until the first is finished, etc.

Thus it is analogous to the behaviour of persons queueing (or 'standing in line', in common American parlance), where the persons leave the queue in the order they arrive, or waiting one's turn at a traffic control signal.

a. Risk management
c. Kanban
b. Trademark
d. FIFO

8. An _____ is a term used in behavioral economics to describe those types of behaviors that impose costs on a person in the long-run that are not taken into account when making decisions in the present. Classical Economics discourages government from creating legislation that targets internalities, because it is assumed that the consumer takes these personal costs into account when paying for the good that causes the _____. For example, cigarettes should be taxed because of the negative consumption externalities that they impose, such as second-hand smoke, not because the smoker harms him or herself by smoking.

a. Inventory turnover ratio
c. Authorised capital
b. Internality
d. Operating budget

9. _____ is generally understood in financial circles as the point at which revenue is recognized, typically through a transaction which involves the exchange of an asset, product, or service for cash or its equivalents.

Chapter 17. Environmental Cost Management 97

This approach gives the accounting division a strictly objective basis for changing the books. For example, a homeowner may believe that his house has grown in value during a strong market, or fallen in value during a weak market, but until the house is actually sold for a specific price to a specific buyer, the change in value can only be estimated and is considered unrealized.

a. Total-factor productivity
c. Merck ' Co., Inc.
b. Valuation
d. Realization

10. The _____ is a performance management tool which began as a concept for measuring whether the smaller-scale operational activities of a company are aligned with its larger-scale objectives in terms of vision and strategy.

By focusing not only on financial outcomes but also on the operational, marketing and developmental inputs to these, the _____ helps provide a more comprehensive view of a business, which in turn helps organizations act in their best long-term interests. This tool is also being used to address business response to climate change and greenhouse gas emissions.

a. Best practice
c. Trustee
b. Management by objectives
d. Balanced Scorecard

11. In economics, _____ or _____ goods or real _____ refers to factors of production used to create goods or services that are not themselves significantly consumed (though they may depreciate) in the production process. _____ goods may be acquired with money or financial _____. In finance and accounting, _____ generally refers to financial wealth, especially that used to start or maintain a business.

a. Disclosure
c. Capital
b. Screening
d. Vyborg Appeal

12. _____ are made by investors and investment managers.

Investors commonly perform investment analysis by making use of fundamental analysis, technical analysis and gut feel.

_____ are often supported by decision tools.

a. Incremental capital-output ratio
c. AIG
b. Investment decisions
d. ABC Television Network

13. The _____ is the United States federal government agency that collects taxes and enforces the internal revenue laws. It is an agency within the U.S. Dept of the treasury responsible for interpretation and application of Federal tax law. The official U.S. Treasury regulations provide (in part):

The _____ is a bureau of the Department of the Treasury under the immediate direction of the Commissioner of Internal Revenue.

a. Income tax
b. Internal Revenue Service
c. Use tax
d. Indirect tax

14. _____ is the process of understanding the stock/product mix combined with the knowledge of the demand for stock/product.
a. ABC Television Network
b. Inventory analysis
c. AMEX
d. AIG

15. A _____ is something that is acted upon or used by or by human labour or industry, for use as a building material to create some product or structure. Often the term is used to denote material that came from nature and is in an unprocessed or minimally processed state. Iron ore, logs, and crude oil, would be examples.
a. 3M Company
b. BMC Software, Inc.
c. BNSF Railway
d. Raw material

16. A _____ is an entity formed between two or more parties to undertake economic activity together. The parties agree to create a new entity by both contributing equity, and they then share in the revenues, expenses, and control of the enterprise. The venture can be for one specific project only, or a continuing business relationship such as the Fuji Xerox _____.
a. Chief Financial Officers Act of 1990
b. Pre-emption right
c. Fraud Enforcement and Recovery Act
d. Joint venture

17. The spot price or _____ of a commodity, a security or a currency is the price that is quoted for immediate (spot) settlement (payment and delivery.) Spot settlement is normally one or two business days from trade date. This is in contrast with the forward price established in a forward contract or futures contract, where contract terms (price) are set now, but delivery and payment will occur at a future date.
a. Market liquidity
b. Financial instruments
c. Spot rate
d. Market price

Chapter 18. International Issues in Management Accounting

1. An _____ is a term used in behavioral economics to describe those types of behaviors that impose costs on a person in the long-run that are not taken into account when making decisions in the present. Classical Economics discourages government from creating legislation that targets internalities, because it is assumed that the consumer takes these personal costs into account when paying for the good that causes the _____. For example, cigarettes should be taxed because of the negative consumption externalities that they impose, such as second-hand smoke, not because the smoker harms him or herself by smoking.
   a. Internality
   b. Inventory turnover ratio
   c. Operating budget
   d. Authorised capital

2. The _____ is the United States federal government agency that collects taxes and enforces the internal revenue laws. It is an agency within the U.S. Dept of the treasury responsible for interpretation and application of Federal tax law. The official U.S. Treasury regulations provide (in part):

   The _____ is a bureau of the Department of the Treasury under the immediate direction of the Commissioner of Internal Revenue.

   a. Use tax
   b. Income tax
   c. Indirect tax
   d. Internal Revenue Service

3. A _____ is an entity formed between two or more parties to undertake economic activity together. The parties agree to create a new entity by both contributing equity, and they then share in the revenues, expenses, and control of the enterprise. The venture can be for one specific project only, or a continuing business relationship such as the Fuji Xerox _____.
   a. Chief Financial Officers Act of 1990
   b. Joint venture
   c. Pre-emption right
   d. Fraud Enforcement and Recovery Act

4. A _____ or transnational corporation (TNC) is a corporation or enterprise that manages production or delivers services in more than one country. It can also be referred to as an international corporation. The first modern _____ is generally thought to be the British East India Company, established in 1600.
   a. Multinational corporation
   b. Privately held
   c. MicroStrategy
   d. Butterfield Bank

5. The _____ is a private, not-for-profit organization whose primary purpose is to develop generally accepted accounting principles (GAAP) within the United States in the public's interest. The Securities and Exchange Commission (SEC) designated the _____ as the organization responsible for setting accounting standards for public companies in the U.S. It was created in 1973, replacing the Accounting Principles Board and the Committee on Accounting Procedure of the American Institute of Certified Public Accountants. The _____'s mission is 'to establish and improve standards of financial accounting and reporting for the guidance and education of the public, including issuers, auditors, and users of financial information.'

   The _____ is not a governmental body.

   a. Financial Accounting Standards Board
   b. Public company
   c. Fannie Mae
   d. Governmental Accounting Standards Board

Chapter 18. International Issues in Management Accounting

6. _____ is subcontracting a process, such as product design or manufacturing, to a third-party company. The decision to outsource is often made in the interest of lowering cost or making better use of time and energy costs, redirecting or conserving energy directed at the competencies of a particular business, or to make more efficient use of land, labor, capital, (information) technology and resources. _____ became part of the business lexicon during the 1980s.
  a. USA Today
  b. US Airways, Inc.
  c. Economic Growth and Tax Relief Reconciliation Act of 2001
  d. Outsourcing

7. _____ is concerned with the provisions and use of accounting information to managers within organizations, to provide them with the basis to make informed business decisions that will allow them to be better equipped in their management and control functions.

In contrast to financial accountancy information, _____ information is:

- usually confidential and used by management, instead of publicly reported;
- forward-looking, instead of historical;
- pragmatically computed using extensive management information systems and internal controls, instead of complying with accounting standards.

This is because of the different emphasis: _____ information is used within an organization, typically for decision-making.

  a. Management Accounting
  b. Nonassurance services
  c. Grenzplankostenrechnung
  d. Governmental accounting

8. _____ refers to a business or organization attempting to acquire goods or services to accomplish the goals of the enterprise. Though there are several organizations that attempt to set standards in the _____ process, processes can vary greatly between organizations. Typically the word e;_____e; is not used interchangeably with the word e;procuremente;, since procurement typically includes Expediting, Supplier Quality, and Traffic and Logistics (T'L) in addition to _____.
  a. Supply chain
  b. Free port
  c. Consignor
  d. Purchasing

9. In monetary economics _____ can refer either to a particular _____, for example British Pounds or United States Dollars, or, to the coins and banknotes of a particular _____, which actually form only a small part of the monetary base of a nation's money supply. The other part of a nation's money supply consists of money deposited in banks (sometimes called deposit money), ownership of which can be transferred by means of checks (cheques in the United Kingdom and Australia) or other forms of money transfer such as credit and debit cards. Deposit money and _____ are 'money' in the sense that both are acceptable as a means of exchange, but money need not necessarily be '_____'.
  a. BMC Software, Inc.
  b. BNSF Railway
  c. Currency
  d. 3M Company

Chapter 18. International Issues in Management Accounting

10. _____ is a form of risk that arises from the change in price of one currency against another. Whenever investors or companies have assets or business operations across national borders, they face _____ if their positions are not hedged.

- Transaction risk is the risk that exchange rates will change unfavourably over time. It can be hedged against using forward currency contracts;
- Translation risk is an accounting risk, proportional to the amount of assets held in foreign currencies. Changes in the exchange rate over time will render a report inaccurate, and so assets are usually balanced by borrowings in that currency.

The exchange risk associated with a foreign denominated instrument is a key element in foreign investment. This risk flows from differential monetary policy and growth in real productivity, which results in differential inflation rates.

a. 3M Company
b. Credit risk
c. Currency risk
d. Market risk

11. In finance, the _____ between two currencies specifies how much one currency is worth in terms of the other. It is the value of a foreign nation's currency in terms of the home nation's currency. For example an _____ of 102 Japanese yen to the United States dollar means that JPY 102 is worth the same as USD 1.

a. Exchange rate
b. ABC Television Network
c. AMEX
d. AIG

12. _____ is a concept that denotes the precise probability of specific eventualities. Technically, the notion of _____ is independent from the notion of value and, as such, eventualities may have both beneficial and adverse consequences. However, in general usage the convention is to focus only on potential negative impact to some characteristic of value that may arise from a future event.

a. Risk adjusted return on capital
b. Discounting
c. Discount factor
d. Risk

13. _____ is activity directed towards the assessing, mitigating (to an acceptable level) and monitoring of risks. In some cases the acceptable risk may be near zero. Risks can come from accidents, natural causes and disasters as well as deliberate attacks from an adversary.

a. FIFO
b. Trademark
c. Risk management
d. Kanban

14. _____ is a term used in accounting, economics and finance to spread the cost of an asset over the span of several years.

In simple words we can say that _____ is the reduction in the value of an asset due to usage, passage of time, wear and tear, technological outdating or obsolescence, depletion, inadequacy, rot, rust, decay or other such factors.

In accounting, _____ is a term used to describe any method of attributing the historical or purchase cost of an asset across its useful life, roughly corresponding to normal wear and tear.

a. General ledger
b. Depreciation
c. Current asset
d. Net profit

15. _____ is systematic determination of merit, worth, and significance of something or someone using criteria against a set of standards. _____ often is used to characterize and appraise subjects of interest in a wide range of human enterprises, including the arts, criminal justice, foundations and non-profit organizations, government, health care, and other human services.

Depending on the topic of interest, there are professional groups which look to the quality and rigor of the _____ process.

a. Evaluation
b. AMEX
c. ABC Television Network
d. AIG

16. An _____ is a classification used for business units within an enterprise. The essential element of an _____ is that it is treated as a unit which is measured against its use of capital, as opposed to a cost or profit center, which are measured against raw costs or profits.

The advantage of this form of measurement is that it tends to be more encompassing, since it accounts for all uses of capital.

a. AIG
b. AMEX
c. ABC Television Network
d. Investment center

17. _____ is one of the four Ps of the marketing mix. The other three aspects are product, promotion, and place. It is also a key variable in microeconomic price allocation theory.
a. Pricing
b. Price
c. Cost-plus pricing
d. Target costing

18. _____ refers to the pricing of contributions (assets, tangible and intangible, services, and funds) transferred within an organization. For example, goods from the production division may be sold to the marketing division, or goods from a parent company may be sold to a foreign subsidiary. Since the prices are set within an organization (i.e. controlled), the typical market mechanisms that establish prices for such transactions between third parties may not apply.
a. Transactional Net Margin Method
b. Pricing
c. Price
d. Transfer pricing

19. The _____ is a performance management tool which began as a concept for measuring whether the smaller-scale operational activities of a company are aligned with its larger-scale objectives in terms of vision and strategy.

By focusing not only on financial outcomes but also on the operational, marketing and developmental inputs to these, the _____ helps provide a more comprehensive view of a business, which in turn helps organizations act in their best long-term interests. This tool is also being used to address business response to climate change and greenhouse gas emissions.

a. Trustee
c. Best practice
b. Management by objectives
d. Balanced Scorecard

20. In mathematics _____s are numbers or other things that get multiplied. In particular, see:

- Factorization, the decomposition of an object into a product of other objects
- Integer factorization, the process of breaking down a composite number into smaller non-trivial divisors
- A coefficient
- A divisor of a particular number, or of an element of a monoid
- A von Neumann algebra with a trivial center

In statistics

- _____ analysis is the study of how _____s or certain variables affect variables.

In technology:

- Human _____s, a profession that focuses on how people interact with products, tools, or procedures
- 'Functionality, Application domain, Conditions, Technology, Objects and Responsibility;', In object-oriented programming

In computer science and information technology:

- Authentication _____, a piece of information used to verify a person's identity for security purposes
- _____, a Unix command for numbers factorization
- _____ (programming language), an experimental Forth-like programming language

In television:

- The O'Reilly _____, an American talk show hosted by Bill O'Reilly on Fox News.
- The Krypton _____, a British game show hosted by Gordon Burns, formally on ITV. Also had an American version.

a. The Goodyear Tire ' Rubber Company
c. Valuation
b. Merck ' Co., Inc.
d. Factor

21. In corporate finance, _____ or _____ is an estimate of true economic profit after making corrective adjustments to GAAP accounting, including deducting the opportunity cost of equity capital. _____ can be measured as Net Operating Profit After Taxes(or NOPAT) less the money cost of capital. _____ is similar in nature to that of calculating another financial performance measure - Residual Income , however, there are a few complexities involved with coming up with the elements for calculating _____ over RI such as the myriad adjustments that might be made to NOPAT before it is suitable for the formula below.

a. International Monetary Fund
b. Outsourcing
c. Internal control
d. Economic value added

22. In finance, _____ also known as return on investment, rate of profit or sometimes just return, is the ratio of money gained or lost on an investment relative to the amount of money invested. The amount of money gained or lost may be referred to as interest, profit/loss, gain/loss, or net income/loss. The money invested may be referred to as the asset, capital, principal, or the cost basis of the investment.
a. Theoretical ex-rights price
b. Debt to capital ratio
c. Capital employed
d. Rate of return

23. _____ refers to the additional value of a commodity over the cost of commodities used to produce it from the previous stage of production. An example is the price of gasoline at the pump over the price of the oil in it. In national accounts used in macroeconomics, it refers to the contribution of the factors of production, i.e., land, labor, and capital goods, to raising the value of a product and corresponds to the incomes received by the owners of these factors.
a. Minimum wage
b. 3M Company
c. Value added
d. Supply-side economics

24. An _____ is a tax levied on the financial income of people, corporations, or other legal entities. Various _____ systems exist, with varying degrees of tax incidence. Income taxation can be progressive, proportional, or regressive.
a. Implied level of government service
b. Ordinary income
c. Individual Retirement Arrangement
d. Income tax

25. In financial accounting, a _____ is defined as an obligation of an entity arising from past transactions or events, the settlement of which may result in the transfer or use of assets, provision of services or other yielding of economic benefits in the future.
a. Corporate governance
b. Vested
c. Liability
d. False Claims Act

26. An _____ is an agreement between a taxpayer and a taxing authority on an appropriate transfer pricing methodology (TPM) for some set of transactions at issue (called 'Covered Transactions'.)

Most _____s involve US taxpayers and the US Internal Revenue Service (IRS), but _____s are also made outside the United States.

Bilateral and multilateral _____sAdvance Pricing Agreements are generally bi- or multilateral--i.e., they also include agreements between the taxpayer and one or more foreign tax administrations under the authority of the mutual agreement procedure (MAP) specified in income tax treaties.

a. Offshore bank
b. ABC Television Network
c. Advance pricing agreement
d. Exchange of information

27. In mathematics, two elements x and y of a set partially ordered by a relation ≤ are said to be _____ if and only if x ≤ y or y ≤ x if and only if x < y or y < x or y = x. For example, two sets are _____ with respect to inclusion if and only if one is a subset of the other.

Chapter 18. International Issues in Management Accounting

In a classification of mathematical objects such as topological spaces, two criteria are said to be _____ when the objects that obey one criterion constitute a subset of the objects that obey the other one .

a. Consumption

c. Comparable

b. Database auditing

d. Scientific Research and Experimental Development Tax Incentive Program

28. _____ in economics and business is the result of an exchange and from that trade we assign a numerical monetary value to a good, service or asset. If Alice trades Bob 4 apples for an orange, the _____ of an orange is 4 apples. Inversely, the _____ of an apple is 1/4 oranges.

a. Price discrimination

c. Discounts and allowances

b. Transactional Net Margin Method

d. Price

Chapter 1
1. d   2. d   3. d   4. d   5. c   6. d   7. b   8. c   9. c   10. d
11. d   12. d   13. d   14. d   15. d   16. c   17. a   18. d   19. d   20. d
21. a   22. c   23. d   24. b   25. b   26. c   27. d   28. a   29. b   30. d
31. d   32. b   33. d   34. d   35. d   36. b

Chapter 2
1. d   2. c   3. a   4. c   5. c   6. d   7. c   8. a   9. d   10. a
11. d   12. b   13. d   14. a   15. c   16. d   17. b   18. d   19. a   20. b
21. c   22. d   23. a   24. a   25. d   26. d   27. a   28. d   29. d   30. a
31. c

Chapter 3
1. a   2. d   3. d   4. d   5. b   6. d   7. c   8. c   9. d   10. d
11. b   12. b   13. a   14. d   15. c   16. d   17. d   18. c   19. d   20. d

Chapter 4
1. d   2. c   3. b   4. d   5. d   6. c   7. b   8. c   9. d   10. d
11. a   12. d   13. d   14. a   15. d   16. d   17. c   18. d

Chapter 5
1. d   2. a   3. d   4. c   5. d   6. c   7. d   8. d   9. b   10. a
11. c   12. a   13. a   14. d   15. d   16. b   17. d   18. d   19. c

Chapter 6
1. a   2. d   3. d   4. d   5. c   6. b   7. b   8. a   9. c   10. a
11. d   12. d   13. d   14. a   15. a   16. d   17. c   18. c   19. d   20. b

Chapter 7
1. a   2. d   3. d   4. c   5. c   6. c   7. b   8. b   9. d   10. d
11. d   12. d   13. c   14. d   15. a   16. b   17. b   18. d

Chapter 8
1. c   2. d   3. b   4. d   5. b   6. d   7. c   8. d   9. d   10. d
11. a   12. d   13. a   14. d   15. d   16. a   17. c   18. a   19. d   20. b
21. a   22. c   23. a   24. b   25. d   26. c   27. a   28. a   29. a   30. d
31. b

Chapter 9
1. d   2. c   3. d   4. a   5. d   6. a   7. d   8. d   9. d   10. b
11. d   12. d   13. d   14. b

ANSWER KEY

Chapter 10
1. d	2. c	3. d	4. d	5. d	6. a	7. d	8. b	9. d	10. d
11. d	12. b	13. c	14. d	15. b	16. b	17. d	18. a	19. b	20. d
21. d	22. d	23. d	24. a	25. d	26. c	27. c	28. a	29. c	30. d
31. d	32. d								

Chapter 11
1. c	2. b	3. a	4. d	5. b	6. d	7. b	8. d	9. d	10. c
11. d	12. d	13. a	14. d	15. d	16. d	17. d	18. a	19. d	20. c
21. d	22. b	23. a	24. a	25. a					

Chapter 12
1. d	2. d	3. d	4. d	5. b	6. d	7. d	8. a	9. d	10. d
11. b	12. d	13. c	14. d	15. d	16. d	17. d	18. d	19. c	20. d
21. c	22. c	23. d	24. d	25. a	26. c	27. b	28. d		

Chapter 13
1. c	2. c	3. b	4. d	5. d	6. d	7. d	8. a	9. d	10. b
11. c	12. b	13. d	14. c	15. d	16. d	17. b	18. b	19. c	20. d
21. a	22. d	23. a	24. c	25. d	26. b	27. d	28. d	29. c	30. c
31. a	32. a	33. d	34. d	35. d	36. a	37. d	38. a	39. d	40. d
41. d	42. b	43. d							

Chapter 14
1. d	2. d	3. a	4. b	5. a	6. d	7. a	8. c	9. c	10. d
11. b	12. d	13. a	14. d	15. c	16. d	17. d	18. d	19. d	20. c
21. a	22. b	23. d	24. b	25. d	26. a	27. d	28. d	29. d	30. d
31. d									

Chapter 15
1. b	2. d	3. b	4. a	5. a	6. d	7. c	8. b	9. c	10. a
11. a	12. d	13. a	14. d	15. d	16. b	17. d	18. c	19. d	20. b

Chapter 16
1. c	2. b	3. b	4. d	5. c	6. a	7. c	8. d	9. d	10. d
11. d	12. d	13. a	14. a	15. d	16. d	17. b	18. b	19. b	20. b
21. d	22. d	23. a	24. c	25. c	26. a	27. a	28. d	29. a	30. d
31. d									

Chapter 17
1. d	2. d	3. d	4. d	5. a	6. d	7. d	8. b	9. d	10. d
11. c	12. b	13. b	14. b	15. d	16. d	17. c			

Chapter 18

1. a	2. d	3. b	4. a	5. a	6. d	7. a	8. d	9. c	10. c
11. a	12. d	13. c	14. b	15. a	16. d	17. a	18. d	19. d	20. d
21. d	22. d	23. c	24. d	25. c	26. c	27. c	28. d